WHAT PEOPLE A

LET YOUR

Drawing on his own deep experience and reflections, along with informed classical sources across most disciplines, David has given us a refreshing understanding of how we and all others may grow in faith, hope and love. The cumulative faith stages will encourage even a beginner in the faith journey.

The text needs careful consideration, alone or in a group, in order to incorporate what we personally need, in our present life experience and context.

Striking quotes include:

"Faith is in essence based upon our emotional and spiritual life ... intellect being secondary"

"All fundamentalisms exhibit spiritual immaturity"

"Where faith development goes wrong or ossifies, personal disaster lurks"

Read unhurriedly, with an intention to act on its wisdom, this book will resource all those poised to dive deeper.

Bruce Gilberd, Bishop Emeritus of Auckland, New Zealand

David Bick is a wise counsellor and a man of great faith. Let Your Faith Grow *will be of great help to many, especially during these times when real faith seems to be a rare and little valued virtue.*

Francis Baird OSB, Abbot of Prinknash

This is a rare, informed synthesis about the growth of faith over the life span by a wise, scholarly Anglican priest with proven experience as a parish leader, pastoral counsellor and spiritual director. His text is alive with biblical, historical and contemporary psychological insights of great worth that can assist in anyone's quest for and deepening practice of faith.

George Carey, former Archbishop of Canterbury

David Bick is a rare, truly attentive listener, a gifted communicator and a wise, insightful, compassionate spiritual director. On meeting him I knew I was in the presence of a holy man, for he bore an 'odour of sanctity'. Let Your Faith Grow *charts that all-important, universal journey of faith, one to help those who are in need of direction or people who are totally lost. I warmly commend this book addressing what Evelyn Underhill terms 'The Mystic Way'.*
Robert Waldron, (Boston, USA), experienced author of spiritual and literary texts

This insightful reworking of Fowler's stages of faith largely from a Christian perspective complements my more secularised update and expansion of the same body of ideas in 'The Psychology of Spirituality' (Jessica Kingsley, London, 2010). I am pleased to recommend this text as a valuable contribution to the increasingly vital and vibrant movement afoot to promote personal spiritual development.
Dr Larry Culliford,Psychiatrist

The nature and nurture of faith charted by David Bick is crucial to human well-being. Combining the fine insights of science and of his own religious tradition (whose Founder's central teachings, rather than frail institutional arrangements of churches, embody eternal, universal truths), he combines psychological insight with practical spiritual wisdom.
Professor Richard Whitfield (Editor)

Reading this manuscript was fundamental in helping me to work through my own faith dilemmas. My faith has not fallen apart, and I can now see that it has been developing, and is still growing, to become more meaningful and real.
Shirley Whitfield, Taken from text in her Foreword

Let Your Faith Grow

Let Your Faith Grow

David Bick

Edited by Richard Whitfield

BOOKS

Winchester, UK
Washington, USA

First published by O-Books, 2011
O-Books is an imprint of John Hunt Publishing Ltd., Laurel House, Station Approach,
Alresford, Hants, SO24 9JH, UK
office1@o-books.net
www.o-books.com

For distributor details and how to order please visit the 'Ordering' section on our website.

ISBN: 978 1 84694 460 4

A CIP catalogue record for this book is available from the British Library.

Design: Stuart Davies

Printed in the UK by CPI Antony Rowe
Printed in the USA by Offset Paperback Mfrs, Inc

CONTENTS

The book cover painting: Light Shining in Darkness, Unquenched, was captured on an autumnal afternoon close by the author's home on the Eastern escarpment above the City of Gloucester. Storm light mysteriously hones in upon the Cathedral tower and those of several adjacent city-centre churches. Signified is a hopeful transformation rather than destruction amid the dark threats of storm, echoing words within the prologue of St John's Gospel (Chapter 1, verse 5).
Richard Whitfield / David Bick

Author's Preface

About a dozen years ago, as my 'retirement' phase loomed (with, for me as a freelancer, no definite bar-lines), I began, spasmodically, to write distillations of my life-learned experience as a pastoral counselor, community leader and teacher. At least a few people with whom I shared early drafts found my writings helpful. Hence as time elapsed I continued, without any particular publishing end in view, though I have often shared these kinds of ideas in talks and seminars, with clients seeking my counsel, and with varied church congregations.

About a year ago I sent text of what I felt was as complete as I could manage to Dorset-based friends who have experienced some of my ministry, the Whitfields. During this spasmodic, latent writing phase, I have retreated briefly on several occasions to their Lyme Regis home for periods of 2 or 3 days each September. Both Shirley and Richard, and others, have encouraged me to turn my written reflections into a book, though to be frank, I did not have the call, contemporary contacts or energy to do so. Hence the project was happily handed over to the Whitfields, and the book you now have in your hands is the outcome.

I know that Richard as my formal editor has not found it easy in devising the chapter structure for the text. Hence I am particularly grateful to him for the format we finally agreed, for his many minor amends to detail, and not least for being able to place the manuscript with a suitable publisher. I also wish to thank Tony Harris for sorting out several 'old' floppy discs on which I had recorded the material for this book over many years of activity, so getting those in a format suitable for Richard to work on.

There are many other people, too many to enumerate by name, who have enabled and enriched my life and faith –

teachers, family, close friends, members of study groups and seminars, and those who have sought my help in distress or for some spiritual direction. I am hugely aware that 'No man is an island'. We are all related to each other in a wide variety of ways, with many permutations and interactions. It is in the patient living out of these inter-dependencies that we grow, develop and learn. Often the one being taught, teaches; and the one being helped enlightens. Such is life's mystery.

Hence I am so thankful for that large network of relationships of which I have been and remain a part, and out of which this book has grown. If any of those people read the text, I hope and expect that they will be able to recognize something that indicates their specific contribution to my words.

David Bick
St Joseph's,
Prinknash Park,
Gloucestershire, UK
GL4 8EU
March 2010

Editorial Perspective

This important rooted and readable book is about the living character of human faith. Crucially, personal 'faith' is not portrayed as some sort of 'once-off' acquisition of a ready-packaged religious creed or secular belief system. Rather, seeds of faith actually tend to grow, change, indeed 'evolve' through particular stages during the human life-course. These relatively unknown phases or 'stages of faith' are the main platform for David Bick's text.

Being invited to edit David's manuscript for publication has naturally required me to continue examining my own periodically stuttering, yet resolute, faith journey. That has brought into fresh focus my diverse, well-motivated prior work and voluntary activities as an often institutionally uncomfortable Anglican laymen. Originally well schooled as a scientist, I observe that faith, which may or may not involve religious belief, is a person's way of inclining into and making personal sense or meaning of life's manifold mysteries. *Faith is of its nature a living dynamic,* an active verb rather than a noun, incorporating systems, images, values and commitments that guide a human life.

David, now in his mid 70s, is an unusual, radical, pastorally-oriented clergyman and grandfather, having long sat lightly with matters of institutional 'church'. He has his roots in the Forest of Dean, a rural region of western Gloucestershire close to the border of England with South Wales. While his earlier parochial ministries have been entirely within his native county, over the past quarter century his influence has spread far wider, and internationally. Over this later period, David has been a truly independent pastor-counselor and teacher. With his wife, Gill, he has resided in a house within the extended community and estate of Prinknash Abbey, a Benedictine monastery, re-established in 1925 after several centuries, about 5 miles from the cathedral city of Gloucester.

After a period of not altogether pleasant National Service in the Army in Malta, North Africa and the Mediterranean area, in which skills learned as a Junior NCO were later to prove formative and valued, David studied at the London College of Divinity. The College was then a School of Theology attached to the University of London, during times of proper respect for original linguistic sources within practical biblical scholarship.

David was ordained in Gloucester Cathedral in 1959, and then served two contrasting curacies, first in St Catherine's, Gloucester, and then in rural parishes clustered around Coleford in the Forest of Dean. During 20 years from 1963 he served as Rector in charge of two different rural regions of the County, including some ongoing responsibilities for the more urban care of people with special social and emotional problems.

In parish life David made himself widely available to both churchgoers and others, including being a community father-figure to many young people. He viewed his parish tasks as being "to inspire and nurture the development of personal faith, and so, through active participation, to enhance personal and social well-being in the natural light of Jesus' teachings." David with Gill are well remembered in their varied roles of teaching, pastoral care, reliable support, and endless, warm hospitality.

However, David often felt deep frustration over what he believed to be a serious waste of his time and energy concerning wider institutional business mediated through Anglican Diocesan structures. Too often he saw those as serious distractions from his vocation to care holistically for people in their particular contexts. He felt (to use his words) "trapped in morass of nothingness of far too much personal posturing and committee work." Hence, in 1983, after various persuasive overtures by the Anglican ecclesiastic hierarchy, yet with the pastoral, but not financial support of his Bishop, David ventured in faith a life of structural independence from his diocese. Welcomed by the Abbot, he de-camped with his family to a bungalow within the grounds of Prinknash Abbey. In taking this step of moving towards independence, with three still growing sons, David was saddened by the lack of seriousness of his Church concerning the 'care and cure of souls', avowedly perceived to be its prime and fundamental charge nationally.

For some two decades before this time, David had become keenly influenced by the exploratory research and teaching of the late Dr. Frank Lake. A pioneering Christian psychiatrist, Lake had founded an independent, non-denominational Christian approach to depth psychology. By 1970 David had become a qualified Regional Tutor within the then Clinical Theology Association. Hence, well before moving to Prinknash, David had been developing new strands of teaching that extended beyond his parish duties. Personal counseling aside, his many geographically dispersed clients included fellow ministers in difficulty.

David's Clinical Theology experience in due course led to two other regular part-time teaching affiliations: one at the University of Bristol Extramural Department; the other at Hawkstone Hall in Shropshire, run under the aegis of the Redemptorist Order within Roman Catholicism, as an ecumenically-inclined international staff training center. Over these times, David did much of his own in-house distribution of teaching hand-outs and booklets, much of this becoming formalized in a now sadly out of print, but widely used book, *Counselling and Spiritual Direction*, Pentland Press, 1997.

I first met David through a series of his 'Clinical Theology' Seminars following those previously taken by my wife, who here contributes the 'Foreword'. Then on the cusp of a conscientious move out of a senior role in the academic system to move into the 'child and family' charity sector, I had no doubt that David was making important practical syntheses concerning faith development and pastoral practice, comfortably tilling much common ground shared by science, the emerging social sciences and theology. En route to his maturity, I know David has assisted many diverse people of varied shades of religious inclination, or none, to iron out creases in their lives, and to sustain them through a wide range of personal crises. He practices what he teaches, being well earthed and well informed, indeed 'streetwise' and non-dogmatic in the best sense of those terms.

In the mid 1980s I encouraged David to write two specific contributions to the marginalized arena of family-based and couple-sensitive learning, touched upon in Chapter 14.

Now David lives in a mature, active non-retirement, suggestively 'an entirement.' He has 'changed gear' appropriately for his stage of faith and life development, staying essentially local for friendly chats with whomever crosses his path, and more than occasional guest church teaching. He is loved by many, not least by his family and grandchildren, and takes his own spiritual practice seriously, meaning that such is no mere habit or obligation, but centers his life.

Here David has distilled much wisdom, his unique text having evolved, like his faith, over many years. It has been my privilege to help bring this practical, well-rooted wisdom to a wider readership that it deserves. My editing of David's text has been detailed but gentle, and all substantive amendments have been thoroughly discussed with him. My main task has been to create a presentational format for enabling his ideas and experience to reach more and diverse readers.

Richard Whitfield, Lyme Regis, July 2010

Richard Whitfield is a Professor Emeritus of Education with a background in both the natural and social sciences. Now Chairman of Trustees of the *Face to Face Trust*, he was successively a Cambridge University Lecturer in Education, Head of Department and Dean of Social Sciences and Humanities at the University of Aston, Director of UK Child Care with Save the Children Fund, and Warden of St George's House, Windsor Castle. He is a latent poet and the author or co-author of well over 30 books, his *Mastering E-Motions: Feeling Our Way Intelligently in Relationship* being published by O-Books.

Foreword

In my late sixties I began to question aspects of my then longstanding Christian faith, one that went back to my early childhood. Beginning to have questions and doubts at this stage of life was very uncomfortable and unsettling.

I am sure that this sort of discomfort can be the case at almost any age, but for me I was questioning the secure beliefs of a lifetime. I felt a mixture of guilt and fear – not least fear that the faith that was mine, and had helped me through difficulties, was about to fall apart.

I became very angry with God, saying that I had not asked for these doubts, and hoping there was divine help that would see me through.

It was suggested to me that I should read James Fowler's *Stages of Faith: The Psychology of Human Development and the Quest for Meaning*. I struggled with the first four parts of that evidence-based book, and then talked with my friend of over 20 years, David Bick, about my dilemmas.

After listening carefully to my plight, David suggested that I might read his then early drafted manuscript for this book, now christened *Let Your Faith Grow*. He explained how his text uses both Fowler's and Erik Erickson's work, alongside his own experience as a priest and counselor, to show how faith can and does develop over a lifetime.

Reading this manuscript was fundamental in helping me to work through my own faith dilemmas. My faith has not fallen apart, and I can now see that it has been developing, and is still growing, to become more meaningful and real. If we get into difficult areas, with this sort of informed help, faith can go on evolving.

Hence I strongly commend *Let Your Faith Grow* to a wide readership.

Shirley Whitfield

[Home-maker, mother, and former primary school teacher]

Chapter 1

Introduction

We all view the world from where we stand. There is no other way because we are all limited by the fact that we are human. In the hearts of all who begin to think and reflect upon life in this world there develops *two kinds of awareness.*

Firstly, how can I cope with all this worldly complexity, which confuses me the more I think about it? *Secondly,* a desire to find some way of understanding that offers a practical method of coping with all that life presents.

Where we stand limits us all greatly in our ability to understand and make sense of our experiences of the world, and in purely human terms, we can do little about it. This leaves us with an ache or angst that longs for a way out, a feeling that beyond the limits of our present environment there must be more, something better; something that enables us to make sense of things, and so get the most out of our present situation. This is in essence some sort of 'spiritual quest' because it must take us beyond the material limits of our existence if pursued to its ultimate end.

This very human situation is at the basis of faith. It is a deep longing in the human soul for fulfillment. It is just there: it being a 'given' of human existence that enables many other things that are creative to happen. Without such sensing we would choke and die in our own frustration and despair. *Faith is a key to living, and is something that, like all other human attributes, needs to be nurtured and developed carefully.*

Those who are lost to this aspect of their humanity through lack of its nurture are greatly deprived, and, at worst, depraved people. Faith can be adequate or inadequate. It can be based upon a false and empty belief, or it can be wholesome and solid with a reliability that is truly freeing. *Where faith development goes wrong, or ossifies, personal disaster lurks.*

1.1 Aims and methods of this book

The summarizing aims of this text are:

- To give insights concerning what faith is.
- To promote understanding of how faith works; and
- How faith can be developed and nurtured over life's course.

Faith is one of the most important things to be understood and developed as far as living a healthy and fulfilled life is concerned, though generally a hugely neglected part of human nurture and development. Education systems mostly fail quite badly in adequately preparing children in this area, and sadly even theological training for those who enter the various ministries in the churches do little better.

I write this text therefore as a contribution towards doing something about such failures, and I have in mind all those who take part in the nurture of others, be they children or adults. I include therefore, parents, teachers, leaders of all faiths and denominations, indeed anyone with any kind of ministry in pastoral care, counseling and spiritual direction, as well as anyone else who can be drawn in. In fact I believe it to be profoundly true that *having a faith and a good understanding of how it works and develops applies to everybody,* though some may not be aware of this.

The method I have chosen in pursuing this study has a twofold basis. The first aspect is an intellectual perspective, involving a little useful 'theory'. The second aspect is that of personal reflection upon my own experiences, both personal in my own faith journey, and also from my experience with other people through well over forty years of ministry as a counselor, pastor and spiritual director, as well as a spouse and parent. I think these two thrusts in an approach to the subject are important in order to achieve balance and understanding. I now develop this further.

The intellectual aspect is practically important in that it provides a degree of objectivity against which one's personal experiences can be assessed. I say 'a degree of objectivity' because, in my opinion, it is impossible for any human being to be totally objective without reducing life to an absurd and meaningless nonsense. When dealing with a subject like faith, this soon becomes clear. Much of the contents of a person's faith are subjective. If this were not so it would simply not work for them. But it is also true that there must be a degree of objectivity in a faith as well, because ***faith** is about putting **trust** in something or somebody outside and beyond ourselves* so that within ourselves we are able to function more effectively as human beings. Simple and totally objectively defined truths, such as two and two making four, are alright in themselves but totally irrelevant when it comes to one's personal well-being and coping with the strains and stresses of daily life.

However, without an intellectually sound theoretical, yet at the same time practical framework, we cannot reflect upon our subjective experiences with any degree of success. All too often in my counseling experience have I struggled with people who become bogged down in their own negative emotional experiences because they lack any well-constructed 'theoretical' framework that enables them to reflect accurately upon the way these emotions are driving them. A theoretical framework, then, is like a basic map that guides us through our subjective experiences. It gives us the equipment we need to understand, interpret and use those within our own growth and development. The 'map' I have chosen for this work is one of 'faith stages' developed by James W. Fowler. I choose this because I think that it is at present the best available. However, I use Fowler's mapping as a framework for understanding, and certainly not as dogma.

What I have just said about the objective theoretical framework is also true in reverse for the experiential, subjective aspect. People cannot live or function on the basis of theoretical knowledge alone, unless one retires, *without returning,* into a very rare and unreal ivory tower, *a risk for all academics*. The arid bones of intellectual understanding become meaningless without the flesh of experience and personal, individualized understanding of that experience.

Second-hand experience has some value, largely as an encouragement. Anecdotal evidence also has its own value, but personal experience within the right kinds of group and social support systems is essential. We all need both to *assemble* and to tell our own faith story using our own experienced personal material. This can only be done successfully when we have both the right sort of theoretical framework and the courage to face our own selves as we truly are; that is where we really are in life, starting from the present moment. *So self-knowledge is very important* in grounding faith. I have therefore included some of my own experiential material, it being part of my own faith journey, and I encourage the reader to do likewise. *My aim is not to write mere knowledge about faith, but to encourage experience and understanding of faith.*

1.2 The structure of the text

The format of the text is one of sectionalized chapters. From this introductory chapter follows a discussion in Chapters 2 to 4 of the nature and character of faith and, importantly, associated issues of prejudice, the phenomenon of human projection, and the role of love in faith development.

Chapters 5 to 11 basically follow James Fowler's scheme of seven 'stages', or phases, of faith development, briefly introduced immediately below, and summarized in Table 1 (page 11). The first stage is an 'undifferentiated' kind of 'pre-stage', being *ideally* one of blissful union between the baby and mother early in life. This is a critical platform for emotional growth and well-being that, in contrast, bad mothering can destroy. Fowler's insightful and suggestive scheme then comprises six further stages. All seven stages run approximately in parallel with the now empirically well-established patterns of life-span psychological development, of which that laid out by the late Erik Erickson is here the most appropriate (see below).

Chapters 5 to 7 cover faith stages that for the most part develop during infancy and childhood. Such foundations are very important because, in my experience of dealing pastorally in depth with a wide range of people, these early stages set underlying patterns for either a good and successful journey through the later stages, or, on the other hand, rather problematical kinds of adult life.

It would seem to be very important that effort is made to lay good faith foundations during childhood because a viable life structure can only be built upon sound foundations. In faith terms, most of later adult faith nurture is about developing what has already been laid down. However, demolishing poor and inadequate early foundations can be a very difficult task; one that needs to be courageously carried through if adult faith is to be appropriately matured in later life.

Chapters 8 to 11 cover the four adult stages of Fowler's scheme, while periodically there is focus upon transitions between faith stages. Chapters 12 to 14 give important reflections upon faith and morality, institutional structures and faith, and, briefly, aspects of family dynamics. Then follows a concluding *Epilogue* (Chapter 15) concerning sustaining faith, hope and love into futures whose detail is unknowable.

Table 1 following summarizes both the structure of the main body of the text, and my principle frames of reference, as now outlined above.

Table 1: Life-course Psycho-social Development and Faith Stages

Life-course phase	Age range (approximate years)	Dipoles of main psychological and social tasks (EH Erikson*)	Faith Stages (JW Fowler**)	Chapters of this book
Infancy	0 to 2	Trust versus Mistrust	Undifferentiated: a 'pre-stage'	5
Childhood	3 to 10	Initiative & autonomy *vs.* Doubt, Shame & Guilt	Intuitive-Projective	6
Early adolescence	11 to 16	Industry *versus* Inferiority	Mythic-Literal	7
Later adolescence	16 to 22	Identity *versus* Role Confusion	Synthetic-Conventional	8
Young adult	23 to 38	Intimacy *vs.* Isolation	Individuating – Reflective	9
Mid-life	38 to 65	Generativity *versus* Stagnation	Conjunctive	10
Old age	65+	Integrity *vs.* Despair	Universalizing	11

*See *Childhood and Society*, Norton, 1963

** See *Stages of Faith*, Harper-Collins, 1981 & 1995

This Table is likely to prove helpful as a summarizing reference during both reading and reflection on the main body of this text. However, *readers are strongly urged not to be distracted at this point by the apparently 'technical' nature of the terms used by either Erickson or Fowler*. At this point, we simply need to recognize that both life and faith evolve through stages, and that such recognition can help us to 'get a life', one of well-being and one worth living!

Throughout the book I approach my text as a practicing Christian, *not because I wish to be exclusive, far from it,* but because that is the underpinning stance from which I have viewed the world for nearly 50 years. It is one with which I am familiar and has brought me great inner peace and fulfillment. But I urge readers to recognize at this point that my own religious faith is in detail very personal, and far from being an early-acquired 'prescriptive package' handed down by 'church authorities', though I am of course greatly influenced by the deepest truths within the balance of Christian tradition, not least the records we have of Jesus' teachings, many of which need skilled interpretation as to their context.

However, I am aware that 'faith' is much wider than any religion, being expressed and experienced in many ways – some of more value than others. Having said this, it is the nature of faith as a thing in itself, and as an essential aspect of being human, that is *my prime concern, not least because all of us are part of a world-wide family manifestly in need of mutual understanding and alive flows of compassionate love.*

1.3 A powerful poetic illustration

Before beginning the task of attempting in Chapters 2 to 4 to set out some kind of adequate definition of what we mean by the word 'Faith', so that a point is established from which an exploration of the subject can begin, I share a Thomas Hardy (1840-1928) poem, *The Dead Man Walking.*

I do this because I believe these few verses, written a little over a century ago in the poet's home county of Dorset show, in graphic terms, the plight of all who have somehow missed out on an adequately nurtured faith. The poem therefore vividly underlines my motivation for attempting this work.

The Dead Man Walking

[by Thomas Hardy]

They hail me as one living
But don't they know
That I have died of late years.
Untombed although?

I am but a shape that stands here,
A pulseless mould,
A pale past picture, screening
Ashes gone cold.

Not at a minute's warning,
Not in a loud hour,
For me ceased Time's enchantments
In hall and bower.

There was no tragic transit,
No catch of breath.
When silent seasons inched me
On to this death...

– A Troubadour-youth I rambled
With Life for lyre,
The beats of being raging
In me like fire.

But when I practised eyeing
The goal of men,
It iced me, and I perished
A little then.

When passed my friend, my kinsfolk,
Through the Last Door,
And left me standing bleakly,
I died yet more;

And when my Love's heart kindled
In hate of me,
Wherefore I knew not, died I
One more degree.

And if when I died fully
I cannot say,
And changed into the corpse-thing
I am to-day;

Yet is it that, though whiling
The time somehow
In walking, talking, smiling,
I live not now.

[From Time's *Laughingstocks and Other Verses,* Thomas Hardy. London: Macmillan and Co. 1909; also see *The Complete Poems,* edited by James Gibson, Palgrave-Macmillan, 2001]

While, like any poem, these lines are open to several interpretations, it is clear that Hardy is expressing the sentiments, indeed tragedy of a lost soul.

A widowed man has said this of the poem:

This poem is the story of my life. When I was young, I was full of energy, and hope and life. Yet, when I fell into that so common relentless competition for income and status, it killed me a little bit. When my friends and family started dying, I died a bit more. When my wife's love for me was gone, I died

> yet more. It is hard to say at what point I was really dead. But I am truly dead now, even though I may look alive to you.

Readers can speculate about this tragic case, and whether, perhaps many times, this man may have shunned or at the very least marginalized matters of encountering faith; of growing faith from prompting seeds that are likely to have presented themselves whether or not he had sampled church or other religiously-related matters. Clearly, materialism's grip, even with some success, had failed to satisfy the man's deep longings. Then, later, he clearly could not cope with loss and bereavement (a tough call for all of us who have felt well-enough connected), his life having become some kind of sad, living form of suicide.

Yet *such a tragic condition need not be*, as we will learn from the rest of this book. Quite simply, all of us at some points in our lives need to pay attention to faith, to personal meaning, and to deeper questions of purpose. Those are fundamental both to and within the 'deal' of being human, and of 'getting a life' more abundant!

Chapter 2

Faith's Nature and Matters of Prejudice

Our first task must be to come to some kind of working definition of what is meant by 'faith'. This is not easy because of the way people use the word and the variety of meanings given to it. For example:

i) Faith could describe adherence to a particular body of doctrine such as those held dear by members of the various Christian denominations, e.g. Catholic, Evangelical, Baptist or Presbyterian.

ii) Faith could describe a person's confidence in a certain kind of medicine or treatment. This is essentially some deeply held personal belief in a treatment's healing powers, usually based upon an individual's own culture or experience; for example, 'a day in bed with a tot of hot whisky beforehand will always cure a cold'.

iii) Faith could refer to belief in a particular political system as a means of curing the world's ills. An example of this is the Marxist belief in the class warfare by which the workers enter into a revolution to overthrow the capitalist system and thereby free themselves and the world from its tyranny. This type of political 'faith' can inspire much commitment and tireless activity among its adherents.

iv) Faith may be a deeply held conviction that a certain way of doing things will always bring about satisfactory results, such as 'If you want a really good cup of tea, always put the milk in first'.

v) Finally, faith could just refer to an attitude of trust in another person. This person could be an authority figure,

> or just a good and kind friend. This wide variety ranges from a doctor, schoolteacher, or parent, to a very well-known and reliable servant or employee. With this kind of trust or faith, the degree of it invested in the person is always relative. For example, it is possible to have a very high level of faith in a person's ability to repair one's car, but that same person might be the last one on earth in whom one would confide. On the other hand, the person whom one would trust most with personal confidences would be the last person on earth to be trusted with the repair of one's car. Here faith is associated with particular competences.

When one reflects upon this variety and complexity of use of the term 'faith', there is one conclusion we can draw with safety. It is that *the way anyone uses the word faith is dependant upon that person's viewpoint*; from where they are in life as far as culture, religion, politics, philosophy and their general situation is concerned. The kind of use we put into the word 'faith' thus originates in our conditioning; and that comes from our whole life experience from conception or birth onwards. In short, *faith is very closely related to 'prejudice'*, and could possibly be seen as a particular kind of prejudice.

2.1 An example of, and exercise about prejudice

I was once preaching on the subject of tyrants. In my sermon I sought to demonstrate that tyrants throughout history shared a common psychology and that this was recognizable, being the same today as it always was. I listed a number of examples beginning in the Old Testament with King Ahab and Queen Jezebel, then Herod and Herodias from the New Testament, followed by a number of examples out of history such as Nero, Henry VIII, Napoleon, Adolf Hitler and Joseph Stalin. After the service a man from the congregation came up to me and was obviously angry. 'That was a very interesting sermon,' he said. 'However, you did make one very serious error.' 'And what was that?' I asked. 'Henry VIII was an Englishman,' he replied most indignantly. No matter what I said to support what I had said from Henry's behavior and the laws he passed, his sole argument was that Henry was English, and all the others were not, with the implication that Englishmen cannot possibly be tyrants, only foreigners can!

One fact of life is that we all have prejudices. This phenomenon is an innate part of being human. Prejudice is something we seem to need in order to make working sense of our lives. This being so, prejudices must just be accepted. Then our problem is one of understanding them, of how they work, and hence appreciating something of both their value and 'down' sides.

Prejudice has a close relationship to faith, but is not identical with it. The man I have just quoted was a very sincere and ardent believer in his country and all the good things he, and people like myself, had inherited just by being born in Britain. He did have a valid point, but his strong prejudice in favor of all things British blinded his awareness concerning other issues.

This raises a very important point about the value of prejudice in its relationship to faith, and that requires further examination, which we will now take up. However, before doing so the reader is invited to do a simple exercise that is aimed at giving us help in becoming aware of our own prejudices.

A simple exercise concerning prejudice

This exercise is very simple, but if taken seriously, can also be very revealing.

In capital letters below I give a number of words. What you do is to look at each word for about a minute, noting your emotional response. Your emotional response is always your first, instant reaction, rather than your considered response. Considered responses cover up what we really feel or think about something, they tend to be what we think is the right, convenient or socially acceptable thing to say. For example, the word 'Margaret' might be the name of a troublesome neighbor whom we find 'a pain in the neck'. Our immediate response to seeing it written down would be something like, 'Not her again', whereas a considered response could well be, 'I should try and be nice to her and not feel such dreadful things. She is my neighbor after all and we should learn to love our neighbor.'

When you have made your emotional response to each capitalized word write it down in a notebook and keep it for future reference. Be very honest expressing what comes to you immediately.

Now here are the 17 words for recording your first, immediate reactions:

MOTHER, FATHER, GOD, SCHOOL, WORK, IRISH, BRITISH, EUROPEAN, BLACK, DANCING, SPORT, FOOTBALL, CRICKET, SUMMER, SNOW, SPRING, POLITICIAN.

Our instant emotional responses to these words give an indication of at least some our prejudices.

After you have written these down it is good to be able to talk openly and honestly about what you have written with someone whom you trust and respect; that is someone who has a good degree of maturity and wisdom who can enter into a dialogue with you, so enabling some self discovery.

It may also be helpful to do this exercise in the context of a small group if it is competently led.*

Footnote

**I mention this because there are too many poorly led groups, in which there is too little awareness of group dynamics. Consequently, people can easily become involved in groups that are likely to do them harm.* (See for, example, section on 'Groups for Emotional and Spiritual Growth' in, *Counselling and Spiritual Direction, D. J. Bick, Pentland Press*).

Becoming aware of our own prejudices is not easy; it takes time, as well as being potentially painful for us. However, this is a most worthwhile activity, and indeed essential if we are to develop a sound and maturing faith.

Having done this exercise, now let us return to our task of formulating a working definition of 'prejudice'.

2.2 Towards a definition of prejudice

The word prejudice means to pre-judge something; to make a decision or draw a conclusion about someone or something without any reference to the objective facts that are presented. It is a purely subjective psychological mechanism. At its worst this can be very dangerous because it distorts the truth. Our response to the daily news as seen on our TV screens and read in the newspapers adequately illustrates this point. Unrecognized and uncontrolled prejudice can cause people to respond to this 'news' in such a way that they draw from it the most outrageous and ridiculous conclusions and then believe them to be true. This inner interpretation of what is presented to us externally is a result of the often unrecognized workings of our prejudices.

Using the activities of prejudice cleverly for their own ends is the stock in trade of all those who seek to manipulate and dominate others, be they dictators, democratic politicians, evangelists, advertising agencies or any form of tyrant it is possible to name. Well worked out punch lines, bold headlines and forceful frequently repeated dogmatic statements sum up the basic method used to hook into people's prejudices. Those cynical about human nature and the world in which we live can easily find evidence to support a viewpoint that sees news, politics or religion as just another saleable commodity, which if packaged cleverly can be sold to anyone with the right prejudices, by people who have the right techniques to do so. Hence the growth of public relations consultancy firms in our time. There is some truth in this because the negative side of prejudice can cause many evils such as bigotry, racial hatred, religious intolerance and a multitude of other things.

One example of this is the use of the term 'Born Again'. This expression became widely used in America by evangelists during the early part of the 20th century to describe those who were converted at their meetings and who rigidly held the doctrines put forward to them. The 'Born Again' person became very fervently committed to a narrow view of the Christian Faith in such a way that all who disagreed with them, even in very minor ways, were just written off as being faithless. From this context the term has now become more widely used, especially in political circles, to describe anyone who has a strong narrow and blind commitment to ideas and beliefs that border on being fanatical and at times ridiculous. Therefore, in common parlance this term carries a generally unpleasant message. It has become shorthand for a narrow-minded, insensitive and unpleasant kind of person.

Now, if we take a look at the origin of this term in St. John's Gospel, we soon become aware that as it was first used it means the exact opposite. I would suggest at this point that the reader looks at St. John's Gospel 1:1–18, and 3:1–21. Read these several times, and ponder on them, coming to conclusions only very slowly and carefully. To me these passages are most profound. Jesus seems to be saying to Nicodemus that he needs to be born again of the Spirit in order to widen his awareness. To allow God's Spirit to change him inside in such a way that he has a fuller life and not a narrower one; to risk living dangerously, and abandon himself a little to the influence of the Holy Spirit over whom a person has no control. It would appear that Nicodemus was aware of a deficiency in his life, and Jesus pointed out that this was a spiritual one which only being born again of the Spirit would cure. The change that this spiritual rebirth would bring was one that would help him give up the need to control, dominate and always have the right answer. It would make him a person of true faith and not one of dogmatic defensive obsessions. In short, it would change his prejudices into being ones that would serve him in a more creative and fulfilling way.

This example shows the two aspects of prejudice and the need to be aware of them. Nicodemus was invited to allow those sets of prejudices by which he made value judgments to be changed so that by their use he could become a better person. Also illustrated is the evils of negative prejudices, how they can distort good things. In my opinion, behind negative projections and prejudices lies the desire to dominate that motivates the lust for power.

It is then of no great surprise that those who are responsible for distorting the original meaning of the term 'Born Again' tend to come from those who are power seekers and empire builders. The evils of such people can more easily be seen by all who do not share their view. It is always those prejudices that are in us, which dominate our lives, which tend to be the worst problem. This is so mainly because we are always to some degree blind to them, and when they are observed by us in others, we can sometimes see them as virtues. Such is the negative side of prejudice, and only when one has gained enough maturity from which to develop the ability to see one's own negative prejudices clearly does one become able to attempt the long process of overcoming them. The exercise which you have just been asked to do is a first step in this process.

2.3 The positive side of prejudice

Fortunately, there is also a positive side to prejudice, which will now be considered. A very wise and experienced school teacher I once knew said to me during a general conversation about parents and children, 'If a parent came to me with a problem about their child, and was not prejudiced in the child's favor, I would be most concerned for the welfare of that child.' This points us directly towards the positive side of prejudice, in that in this type of case it arises out of love. The parent who truly loves its child will identify most strongly with it in terms of the child's real needs as a person. This kind of prejudice is an essential factor in the child's nurture. This is so because it helps the parent not to project their own needs, desires or ambitions onto the child. Genuine love can never impose anything on a child or any other person. True-love supports, encourages, disciplines, yet also gives freedom for the dependant person's growth into maturity and healthy independence. There is, however, a problem here because love is a very complex thing. It is something that we have to learn about by being loved by others before we can become a person who can love someone else. It has in its fullness both a human, down to earth dimension as well as a transcendent other-worldly dimension. Love is also something that is not static, but growing and developing, always needing nurture from sources outside us that are not exhaustible by our demands.

At this point I would suggest that the reader takes time to ponder upon St. Paul's First Letter to the Corinthians, chapter 13 (with which my text ends – see page 231). This I consider to be the finest definition of the true nature of love in the whole world.

Returning to the issue of parental love needing to be positively prejudiced in favor of the child, this parental love shown through a mother, and also generally by any loving parent, is not all that is required for love and care that nurtures into maturity. The influence of other people who care in different ways is of equal importance. The statement made by the teacher to which I have referred is wise because it sees as creative the prejudice of the parent in terms of providing the basis for a dialogue which could lead to furthering the child's nurture and development. Were it possible for the parent to enter into a full and balanced dialogue with the teacher about the child's problem, it would enable other important things to happen. Because the teacher does not have the same kind of prejudiced attitude as the parents, a healthy degree of professional objectivity would be introduced into the dialogue. The interaction between the two standpoints taken in this dialogue, which for the sake of this argument could be called the prejudiced/ emotional (parent), and the rational/objective (teacher), would be more likely to arrive at some solution beneficial to all concerned.

On the other hand a dialogue that ended in a head-on clash in which the parent felt the teacher to be unsympathetic and anti-child, and the teacher feeling the parent to be a crazy, irrational over-protective idiot, would only serve to re-enforce the existing prejudices of both parties and be very detrimental to the nurture and development of the child. The chances are, in such a case, that the child would also develop some negative prejudices of its own that would be carried into adulthood.

From this we can see how prejudices are developed in both positive and negative ways. It also shows that they are also greatly influenced in their development, not only by significant early personal relationships, but also through the influence of a variety of social interactions that take place within the wider society in which we are nurtured as children. These influences are very complex and not always obvious, but they all contribute towards forming an environment, or 'culture' in which young and developing people have prejudices formed within them that set up definite patterns of behavior and belief systems for the future.

Influences of this kind that are for good can only come out of situations in which there are understanding relationships, both between the child and adults and also between the adults in the child's life, to set up personal experiences and models of behavior that create positive prejudices within the child. For example, good experiences of teachers in which there is a high degree of understanding, fairness, discipline that creates security, and a general sense of well-being, in which pain and other difficult situations are faced with appropriate support given, will develop positive prejudices towards teachers and schools in general. A *fantasy image** will develop in the child's mind in such a situation by which all teachers and schools will be deemed to be good automatically. Therefore, the non-rational premise taken by such a person in adult life, upon which all other reasoning on this subject is developed, will be that all teachers are basically OK people, and those who are not must be 'exceptions to the rule'.

In cases where the majority of such experiences are negative, then the opposite will be true, because a negative fantasy which pictures teachers in a bad light will become established in the child's mind that is destined to govern its thinking in adult life. This can be applied to the whole of life. For the word 'teacher' we can substitute: mother, father, family, doctor, police, men, women, race, color or religion, in fact just about everything that is experienced in formative relationships during our early years.

The formation of prejudices is more powerful in childhood than in later life, but they continue to be formed throughout our lives. They can also be changed and reformed given the opportunity and right environment, but this is not easy and requires the will to attempt it on behalf of the individual. There are useful ways in which this can be achieved by the use of 'Fantasy Journeys',* which will be considered in more depth at a later stage.

Footnote

** The important part fantasy plays in our development and its role in helping us to cope with the problems we face in everyday life, as well as being able to come to a satisfactory understanding of them, is dealt with by Julia Segal in her book: 'Phantasy in Everyday Life'. For practice see also my short pamphlet on 'Fantasy Journeys' and how to conduct them.*

In this very simple explanation I have just outlined extremes, because to do this makes understanding the principles involved easier. It is however, important to point out, that for most of us our prejudices are a much more complex mixture of positive, negative and somewhere in-between, which needs a great deal more sifting and sorting than could be deduced from the simple illustration I have used here. However, we have now reached a point at which it is possible to formulate a rough and adequate working definition of what is meant by the word 'prejudice', and need to do so if only for the purpose of enabling ourselves to move on in our perceptual understanding.

2.4 Summarizing elements within perceptions of prejudice

Concerning prejudice, four elements of summary can now be articulated.

i) Prejudice encompasses those assumptions from which a person begins the process of giving meaning to their everyday experiences of life; the touchstone on which experiences are tested, interpreted and given value.
ii) From this it automatically follows that prejudice invariably forms the premise or starting point from which discussions and arguments take place.
iii) Prejudice has its basis in our fantasy world. This 'Fantasy World' consists of a large and varied number of images built up over the years from all that we have ever experienced, whether good or bad, pleasant or painful. These are stored away within the depths of our being and used as a reference point in understanding and interpreting all further experiences we might have. This happens automatically in a subconscious way and determines our response to people and situations.
iv) Our prejudices therefore work like an automatic pilot, directing us in ways of which we are almost totally

> unaware. They are indeed useful in enabling us to cope with living, but they do need to be understood and carefully developed. Their value is that they are very energy saving. We can use them to make those many decisions that have to be made in the course of everyday living in the same way that an airline pilot uses the automatic pilot. They do many things for us automatically and save us from having to dither or agonize in a 'Should I or shouldn't I, can I or can't I' energy-draining way over many issues.

However, just like the automatic pilot, if our prejudices are misplaced, faulty or badly adjusted we can crash or get into serious trouble. To be inner-balanced as a person, we need to be aware of this and give adequate attention to the correction and adjustment of our prejudices for the whole of life.

Chapter 3

The Phenomenon of Human Projection

Having looked at how prejudice features in the development of faith, any faith, we must now turn our attention to another hugely influential psychological mechanism, common to us all, that works in conjunction with prejudice in the exercise and development of faith. This is *projection*. Projection is a subconscious activity which attributes to other persons feelings and characteristics which one has inside oneself, yet cannot recognize or accept as being a negative aspect of oneself; *or* positive characteristics and qualities in others which one desires but does not have oneself.

It is more in this second sense than the first that we see it operating in conjunction with prejudice in the process of faith development. The negative aspect of projection happens to be the cause of scapegoating and demonizing of individuals and groups of people whom we find threatening. It can be observed in the negative aspects of any faith system which declares 'them' as being evil, the enemy or destructive of true faith.

However, at this stage we must put this negative aspect to one side and follow up the positive side of projection. This lies at the root of hero worship and idealism and is easily observed in the young, developing person. As with prejudice, positive projections are quite complex and not always easy to recognize. All this is another intrinsic part of being human, and also, in common with prejudice, it is a need we all have. It is capable of being both good and positive or negative and destructive in our relationships with others and our development as balanced human beings. It could be said that the main reason for projection lies in the fact that we are limited, finite beings, with a deep inner need, that is not always recognized, to reach out to something beyond ourselves. Failure to do this, together with not being able to make some kind of meaningful contact 'out there', leaves us with a sense of feeling something less than we really are, yet at the same time not often understanding what it is. We can frequently observe this in people whom we describe as 'seeking for something'.

The practice of projection goes on continuously through our lives, but it tends to be more powerful when we are young. It is largely an unconscious process. Because of its automatic nature, it is possible for some people who do it all the time to be totally unaware of this until something happens in their life that forces the habit upon their attention, thereby thrusting them into a new awareness. This 'not knowing' is not necessarily a bad thing. When life goes well within the context of sufficiently good and supportive relationships, and certain values and other basic needs are always there, all that which makes for a viable lifestyle becomes taken for granted. When all we need for a good, or even adequate life, is in place, and as a result of this we are happy, there is no deep need to question anything.

This 'no need to question anything' attitude, together with a non-awareness of projection, is in fact an attitude of simple basic faith. It comes about because in such cases all the unconscious projections are functioning to enable a viable or even good and happy lifestyle to be lived.

It is only when our unconscious projections do not work in this satisfactory manner that our sense of well-being becomes threatened, and we are forced by necessity to do something to calm our inner 'dis-ease', that questioning and reflection take place. This involves gaining an awareness of our projections and other factors involved in a living faith. But these only tend to become seriously exposed to us when that living faith ceases to be viable.

This process of 'losing faith' will be looked at in detail when we later examine faith development stages at the core of this book. We simply need to note here that loss of faith in one set of objects or persons, onto which workable projections were made, is part of a process of growing and maturing faith. It is mentioned now because it involves our projections, and I believe that it shows how much they are an essential part of a person's practical working faith. In St. Matthew's Gospel 10:19, Jesus Christ is recorded as saying: 'Anyone who finds his life will lose it; anyone who loses his life for my sake will find it.' Here, we reasonably take 'life' to mean 'faith'. This shows that *faith of any kind that is deepening and real must involve a continuing process of loss in order to gain it in a deeper way*. Such faith is not static and fixed, but dynamic, changing, and potentially growing.

Now, I think it is possible to see how projection is an important aspect of faith that we tend not to notice, until that in which we have faith fails us. The relationship between prejudice and projection can also now be more clearly understood. In this relationship it would appear that our *prejudices are largely responsible in determining the form our projections take, and towards whom or what they will be directed.*

The simple Table 2 here (page 31) sets out principles involved in the prejudice-projection relationship. The reality is more complex, and like all simplifications should not be taken literally, but used as a summarizing guide.

Table 2: Depicting relationships between prejudice and projection in the varied processes and stages of faith development

Negative side Used to direct projections onto objects or people we perceive as being bad, so helping us to cope with our inwardly-felt pains.	**In the middle,** inside our soul-centers	**Negative side** Used to direct projections onto objects or people we perceive to be desirable, yet which we feel we probably lack.
God	Held within us are all our *prejudices* formed during our past and present *nurture*. These are used to direct our *projections* onto what we perceive to be relevant.	God
Men		Men
Women		Women
Children		Children
Sports-people		Sports-people
Artists & celebrities		Artists & celebrities
Parents		Parents
Authority		Authority
Evil		Goodness

Some will find this Table helpful. However, others might see it as being irrelevant or even a hindrance to their understanding. We need to remember that we are all very different in our methods of communicating and understanding.

Chapter 4

The 'Third Factor' of Love in Faith Development

Having looked at the place of *prejudice* and of *projection* and their relationship to each other in the process of faith development, we must now give some attention to what I call the 'Third Factor'. In short, using one word only, this is ***love***. However, this small four-letter word is used to describe something that in its fullness is indefinable. We can experience love in many ways and at many levels. For example, both C.S. Lewis' 'Four Loves' and Eric Fromm's 'The Art of Loving', give us an indication of love's complexity. Nevertheless, both fine books come from the same direction, one of showing how human beings experience love in different ways, and that these are essential factors within our personal growth, development and well-being.

My editor (in his O-Book *Mastering E-Motions: Feeling Our Way Intelligently in Relationship*) has written of differing types or forms of love, each with early Greek or Latin names:

(a) *filio*: brotherly or sisterly friendship and companionship love;
(b) *eros*: sexual affection, passion or desire;
(c) *storge*: a warm affection or liking; and
(d) *agape*: an unselfish and unconditional caring for another person's whole being, in which the lover's own need for love is secondary.

To these can be added:

(e) *ludus*: playful, or teasing forms of love;
(f) *mania*: an obsessive and so possessive kind of love; and
(g) *pragma*: a calculating, manipulative type of love.

Richard goes on to contrast romantic love with binding friendship love, properly noting that the *agape* form of love is by far the deepest variant, strongly associated with the Christian tradition. Agape is essentially a 'gift-love', one twinned with compassionate commitment and promising. This for many, at least in previous eras, was termed 'a covenant'.

I wish to say at the outset that love is a very great mystery. By using the word mystery we enter the world of true religion, because a mystery is something we human beings can never fully understand, define or control. We can experience it, grapple with it, and even come to an understanding of it in a partial way that is wholly satisfying to our present situation and condition, endowing a sense of inner peace and well-being, while at the same time leaving us with a sense that there is always more to experience. The best description of this that I know (and noted previously on page 23) is in 1 Corinthians, chapter 13 (see page 231). This can be read many times over without ever exhausting its spiritual content.

At this point, enough has been said about this 'Third Factor'. Now I will endeavor to give a practical example of how it works in conjunction with both personal prejudice and projection. My example concerns the widely experienced phenomenon of '*Falling in Love*'.

When a 'falling in love' happens between two people, generally of opposite genders, what we observe is most interesting from the point of view solely of the projections and prejudices involved. The initial factor is a mystery, it just happens out of the blue. In the common parlance of today it would be said that 'the chemistry' is right between these two people, but I consider this far too simplistic and demeaning of such a powerful and great mystery. It is wiser to accept it as a great and powerful wonder of our existence that is an enriching and life-giving experience, which we can enjoy. Our task is to manage the experience properly, respect and value it knowing that, like a beautiful and delicate plant, the top priority is its secure nurture.

From this starting point the psychological process that is set in motion as a result of falling in love in the first place is something we can observe, and learn from, as an aid to its sustenance and development. In short, we must accept the mystery of love as something great and powerful that sets depth movements in motion and can be seen as having certain psychological processes that seem to cause or allow it to happen, but in essence it is bigger than and beyond all these processes. Now let us look at these processes.

It is often observed that, despite many external appearances, a woman tends to fall in love with a man who is similar to her father, and likewise a man with a woman similar to his mother. This is not always the case, but quite frequently so. As a result the expectations each has of the other are similar to those already established within the woman by her relationship with her father, and by the man in his relationship with his mother. In this example we see how prejudice and projection work together. In both of them the imprint of their previous experience and nurture sets up strong patterns of relating to the opposite sex.

From this starting point the power of the love that brought them together in the first place needs to be strong enough to form a basis from which both of them can iron out the elements of prejudice and projection that are not helpful to the development, well-being and day-to-day practical functioning of an evolving relationship. This process of development needs to take place if both are to be fulfilled, and it can involve a very painful struggles at times. Relationships are by their very nature dynamic, alive and always developing. If this is not recognized and fully understood, our relationships stagnate and die. The experience of love must be such that it motivates the process of adjusting to the realities of the accompanying prejudices and projections.

In a committed relationship the process of re-adjustment is a continuous one, enabling each partner to discover the real person in their partner that lies behind the projections. This 'real person' is never fully perceived at the beginning of a relationship. From this fact it follows that there must be a need for an honest examination of the expectations each one puts upon the other, and also a recognition and acceptance of the genuine needs of the other person in the relationship. These factors are always ongoing and present in the everyday 'here and now' affairs in the relationship. For love in relationship to grow and develop satisfactorily these things must be disentangled from the prejudices and projections rooted in each person's past. Without this taking place, no relationship can survive in a fulfilling state, and the love (rather than possible infatuation) that enabled the relationship to happen in the first place will become stifled.

This now brings us to the point where we can draw out a few important matters about the relationships between prejudice, projection and faith.

4.1 Relationships between prejudice, projection and faith

i) These three phenomena work together in every person. They condition each other, so cannot be treated as totally separate entities.

ii) They enable relationships to be initiated, but for good relationships to be sustained, factors that are beyond them need to be discovered and accepted. The fact is that, whatever the overlapping characteristics and easy compatibilities, there is another person with their own characteristics who exists in their own right, beyond that which is perceived through our prejudices and projections. This reality needs to be discovered, and this process of discovery takes time and patient effort.

iii) Therefore, a relationship can only grow and develop successfully if a truly sustained and sometimes painful process of learning and readjustment takes place. For this to happen, commitment and sensitivity within struggle are essential.

iv) Faith essentially forms and grows from *relationship*. Therefore all that applies to developing and sustaining a human relationship also applies to faith.

v) Sexuality is involved in relationship and personal development, and is also involved in faith. This is ever present, too often controversially, throughout the history of the Christian Faith. In the New Testament the relationship between the believer and Jesus is likened to that between the bridegroom and the bride. The Christian mystics frequently talk about their relationship with Jesus Christ in terms of lover and loved one. A good example of this is within the book by a modern mystic Gabrielle Bossis entitled *'He and I'*. This is compatible with the whole history of Christian mysticism; this theme being found in the later Old Testament writings such as the 'Song of Songs'.

It has just been demonstrated by the use of the above simple illustration how both prejudice and projection work together in the process of building up faith in another person or object outside oneself. This is based upon what is known as 'Object Relations Theory' in the world of psychology, and is rooted in the work of Freud but has been developed by others both in Britain and America. Most notable people in this development are Fairbairn, Guntrip and Winnicott.

The basis of ORT is that relationships with significant people, especially the mother, during infancy and our formative years, set up responses, patterns of behavior and quite complex inner emotional mechanisms by which we understand and interpret all our subsequent relationships. This theory relates the subjective (i.e. those things which go on inside a person), to the objective (i.e. those things which happen in the world outside the individual person).

I find Object Relations Theory very interesting in the way it relates to theology, both at the level of scripture and of classical theology such as the Ontological Argument for the Existence of God, as put forward by Anselm in the 11th century. The key point is that in the relationship between psychology and theology, both say that what goes on inside a person is directly related to what goes on in the world outside them, especially during their formative years. As a result of this, their ability to perceive and understand the world around them for the rest of their lives is conditioned by this early formation. Therefore our perceptions of our external world are always conditioned by how we experienced it in our early years.

The first cause of our existence is external to us, through the immediate coitus of our biological parents, but ultimately 'God'. As our parents are immediate, or the first cause as far as the infant's experience is concerned, our relationship with them will have a great influence on our relationship with God, especially in our early years. A good early relationship with parents (biological or adopted) is therefore a very good launch-pad from which an evolving, relaxed rather than rigid relationship with God can be developed in later life.

However, it would not be sufficient for us to leave it here. Such an illustration does give us a fundamental model upon which further understanding can be based, though such must not be pushed too far. It is also essential to look at other ramifications that are involved, emphasizing the fact that our main concern is a purely practical one, for which I am seeking to establish a suitable working model. I next attempt to do this.

4.2 Three further considerations

4.2.1 Paranoid tendencies

The first further consideration is the use of prejudice and projection to deal with any evil that a person perceives as being a threat to their well-being in either an actual or imagined way.

When this happens, certain people or objects are perceived as being bad and must be avoided or opposed at all cost. In times of war or personal conflict they are the enemy, and so must be defeated. In such cases, each 'side' sees itself as being good and the other as being bad. Everything becomes absolute, and the greater the perceived threat, the more dogmatic is the stand taken against it. In an individual person, the same process takes place when hurt or threatened by other people. In extreme cases, where severe deprivation has been experienced, especially in infancy, it is used to ease emotional pain that is too hard to bear, by projecting it onto other people, situations or objects. This is the cause of 'paranoid' behavior, something from which none of us is exempt at times of crisis in our lives.

There is, however, one big problem with paranoid behavior. This is graphically summed up in a commonly used saying, 'Just because you feel paranoid it does not mean that they are not getting at you.' The simple fact is that we get the same feelings when someone is really trying to undermine or destroy us as we do when, due to past hurts that cause neurotic behavior, we are made to feel that people are against us when they are not.

In order to get things into balance we need to bear in mind two issues. The first is the need for a sufficient degree of objectivity about the perceived danger, and the second one is to do with our own personal growth and awareness. When these two factors are present we will be able to discern whether or not any perceived danger or evil is dangerous, or evil in its own right and not just a distortion in our perception. When both our perceptive inner mechanisms work accurately because they are not being distorted by our neuroses, and we are able to evaluate with a good degree of objectivity the warning feelings that signal danger, we will not behave in a paranoid way. Whenever these two things are not present or functioning adequately, then we will become easily subject to paranoid behavior.

It is then easy to see from this how and why demonologies are created. It is a form of paranoia, coming from our need to defend ourselves so that we will not be destroyed. It is a distortion of something natural and healthy that all human beings have, which only becomes 'sick' or paranoid when people are not adequately nurtured or even aware of their spiritual and emotional needs.

There may or may not be a threat or demon, therefore the prejudice-cum-projection technique on its own neither validates or invalidates the objective reality of a threat or demon. It merely records a process of response that happens to be an emotional factor common to all people. Objective validation of a perceived external threat or demon requires something else of an empirical nature. This is the realm of value judgments, because the same psychological process that enables us to relate to objects of faith also has the same function in enabling us to relate to evil and demonologies. This is another issue that we must take up again later.

4.2.2 Absolutist and fundamentalist thinking

The second 'further consideration' follows on from this. It is about the origins of this very black and white approach that has just been stated, and which is also evident in people who are behaving in a paranoid way. This kind of behavior is unhelpfully regressive. It originates approximately from the age between two and four years. During this time of life, our fantasy world is at its highest level of activity, and the world in which we live is being explored and understood almost entirely by this means.

Projection is the main tool used at this phase, and everything is animated by the imagination prior to it being understood in terms of how it affects the youngster's well-being. That which hurts and frightens is bad, and that which makes one feel happy and an OK person is good. Faith or trust is put in that which is experienced as good, and mistrust in that which is experienced as being bad. At this stage of our development lie not only the roots of faith and trust, or of mistrust and non-faith, but also the empirical basis for personally testing these. This whole process is, however, very embryonic, but it does set up criteria that determine manners of personal development which will be looked at later.

4.2.3 Towards a valid basis of faith

The third 'further consideration' is about testing the validity of what or whom we decide to invest our faith in, by use of the prejudice and projection technique. As we have seen, at the point of origin our means of testing objective value are very limited, or indeed almost non-existent, but as we get older they do develop. This takes place mainly in two areas, our personal experience; and the developing modes of operation of our intellect, that is our rational thinking. The latter gives us means whereby, in the absence of emotional turmoil, we can reflect upon the material that is supplied by our everyday experience and carefully evaluate it.

We have now become aware of the basic psychological factors that underlie the development of faith in a human being. This process would indicate that *faith is to do with a deep human need for us to fulfill ourselves by projecting onto people and other objects outside ourselves properties, values and meanings that we desire,* in order that this fulfillment might be achieved. It is also, at a lower level, something we need to do so that we can cope with everyday living in some kind of meaningful way.

We have also seen that this process begins in infancy, or even before, from conception. This develops all through our lives, continually being tested by the dual means of experience and an intellectual type of reflection. At certain times meaning and significance can be lost, rediscovered in another form, or transferred onto another person or object. There is also a dark or negative shadow side, that which is experienced as being 'bad'.

When tested and valued as such, this tends to be demonized or put in the category of being evil. This is an element in moral development which is also a continual process that arises out of faith. That which enhances and develops the person has the moral value of being good, and that which destroys is evil.

This point raises the big issue of relativity in moral values because the whole argument we have followed so far would indicate relativity insofar as that which might destroy a person at one stage of development would not do so at a more advanced stage. I think this is true, but not the whole truth about morality because some values must be absolute or infinite in order that the finite or developing might have points of stability that enable growth. The only emphasis I would want to make here, for the purpose I set out to achieve, is that moral development and awareness always grow out of faith. Therefore, to develop and understand faith is essential for the development of a sound morality.

It seems to me that the stand Jesus took against the Pharisees in the Gospels was all about this issue. They tried to impose a morality on people without doing anything to nurture faith. (See St. Matthew, chapter 23, on the seven 'woes' to the Pharisees.)

All these things are aspects of faith present in one form or another all through our lives. Like an arm or a leg, faith in all these varied aspects is an integral part of being human. We can only gain moral awareness, a sense of what is right and wrong, in relationship to our development as whole. It is from this starting point that we now go on to explore the nature of faith in greater depth, looking at its growth and evaluating its varied kinds of expression at different stages of its development.

Chapter 5

Stage 1 – An 'Undifferentiated' Phase of Faith in Infancy

5.1 Growing up into faith

It is an easily observable fact that everyone grows old, and as we grow old we change. The physical changes are very obvious, but the emotional and spiritual changes are less so. It is not that these last two are not easy to observe, but that they are more complex. Old people can behave emotionally as if they were younger, and some young people can behave as if they were old, even though in physical terms they may 'look their age'. Some very competent or highly intelligent adults can in some situations behave as irresponsibly as a child or adolescent. There are also those who hold very high responsible jobs in public life, but in their private life and personal relationships are highly incompetent, so dysfunctional.

These observations point us to one important factor that must always be taken into account when we seek to understand how people tick. It is simply that *chronological age is not an indication of maturity or of emotional and spiritual development*. Those are two different things, but have a relationship which lies mostly in the sphere of opportunity. A 10 year old just has not had the same chance as a 60 year old to experience life, but a 60 year old may not have made much at all within those years of experience in terms of their emotional and spiritual growth.

This is all true of faith because our faith is in essence based upon our emotional and spiritual life, with the intellect being a secondary factor. Just as highly competent and intelligent people can be childish, incompetent and immature in their private lives and personal relationships, so also can such people be immature and lacking in matters of faith. Many people involved in counseling, pastoral care and spiritual direction have observed and commented upon this throughout history. In general, *the problem of faith not being developed in parallel to physical and emotional growth is one of nurture and social values.*

In a very materialistic society, giving time and effort to faith development does not appear to matter much because the skills required for earning a good living and 'getting on' in this world become all important. In this kind of social climate faith is not nurtured, and where it is taught it often becomes so intellectually based that it is reduced to a kind of religious knowledge shorthand. 'We have done all that,' people say, 'and now I can get on with living in the real world.' But what is not appreciated is that they have not even begun to understand faith's nature.

I have found through my experience that there are basically three ways in which such lack of understanding about faith and its nurture manifest themselves.

5.1.1. Changes in attitudes and needs

I begin with this aspect because it applies to those who have a recognized and workable faith, but because of the way they now feel about the external expression of it, they are becoming concerned. Practical examples of this are (and I quote):

(a) 'I used to love singing choruses and going to lots of meetings, but now I am bored with them and at times feel hostile to the people who seem to be enjoying them like I used to.'

(b) 'I now hate all the noise and fuss the campaigners make. I used to enjoy all the excitement of protesting and organizing marches etc, but now I just want to be quiet. Being like this makes me feel guilty because I ought to be making some effort.'

(c) 'I thought I had my life up-together, but now I am not so

> sure. I get the weirdest dreams and they frighten me. I also feel that I would like to go away where I am not known and start all over again.'

These are but three general examples of the kind of things that have been said to me over the years. I have also felt them myself. They are always said by people roughly between the chronological ages of 30 and 50. In my studies of spiritual writings from the past I have seen that what I was observing was a *natural* change in the outward expression of a person's faith and a corresponding change in the requirements for its ongoing nurture. It would appear that there is a marked change that comes somewhere in middle life from the need to take an active stance, to the need to take a more passive one in the expression and nurture of personal faith.

5.1.2. Loss and re-discovery

Losing faith in God, or whatever else one believes in, is a very common thing. It is always traumatic, and because of this many people now seek counseling at these times of their life. I include the word 're-discovery' here because we all need to have faith in something, and so the loss of faith in one object always includes the gaining of faith in another, even though the re-discovery is not always recognized for what it is. This 'loss and rediscovery' process is a natural part of faith development and takes many different forms. The most important issue is the conscious realization that this is what is happening. Its pain must never be avoided, and must be lived through. For this reason the support of a competent person who takes the role of 'soul-mate' and enabler is important.

5.1.3. Stuck people

These are those whose faith development is stuck at a point well behind their chronological age and/or intellectual development.

The cause of this is always inadequate nurture. The inadequacy takes two extremes. The one is that of intellectual avoidance, where mature people in chronological terms and worldly ability just have not used their minds to test out their faith, and end up trying to live out a faith lifestyle that is in tension and conflict with their environmental experience. They tend to resort in ridiculous ways to deny the very real problems that need to be faced.

The other extreme is the very intellectually competent person who is so immature emotionally, inwardly very frightened and inadequately nurtured emotionally, that they have no awareness at all of the existence of that vast area of life that is non-intellectual. Such people use their intellect to deny anything that might not fit easily into the way they would like to perceive the world, and in so doing are forced into trying to live out a very vulnerable and easily threatened lifestyle.

There are of course many other variations of this that fall between these two extremes, but the point at issue is the same. These folk are all very firmly stuck in their faith development at a point well behind that at which a better nurtured person would be at the same chronological age.

5.2 Returning to Fowler's 'Seven Stages of Faith'

Having made these general observations by way of introduction, let us now look in more detail at this issue of faith development. In order to do this, as intimated in the second section of Chapter 1, I propose using the framework provided by the work of J.W. Fowler, which I believe to be the most comprehensive yet done in this area. I will illustrate and enlarge on this from my own experience. In this connection, readers will find Table 1 (page 11) showing seven stages of faith, helpful en route through this and later chapters.

Faith stages in Fowler's scheme are, as we have seen, directly related to the stages of human emotional development as set out by Erickson, and broadly confirmed by many other scholars. Faith is not necessarily a faith in God, but a faith in an external object, person or projected ideal.

However, as I have intimated, I write from the basis of faith in God (or 'Divine One') because I both believe and experience that ultimately this is the only fully satisfying and complete form of faith. This scheme of Fowler's does not concern itself with the nature of the object of faith, or with any kind of formal theology, but only with the way in which the faith is expressed and lived out in a person at any particular stage of their development. Its value is that it tells us roughly where we are, faithwise, so that when this is perceived we are able more accurately to prescribe for ourselves, possibly in discussion with a pastoral counselor whom we respect, appropriate new means of nurture for encouraging maturing change, as well as having a greater understanding of our whole selves.

5.3 Stage 1: A phase of 'undifferentiated' faith

This is the infancy stage, and if faith is to become real it grows alongside the natural trust a baby has in its mother. This is a preverbal and pre-intellectual stage of development in which the tiny person does not know itself as an individual that has a separate existence apart from its source of being, who is mother. At this stage the person and object of faith are one. Where this 'Oneness' is able to continue without being broken during the necessary period of nurturing time, then feelings of well-being, hope, and, above all, trust develops in the infant.

As this infant grows older and develops, this trusting attitude predisposes them towards faith of a positively trusting kind. If the nurture is not adequate, then they are predisposed towards mistrust, and faith in others becomes more difficult. This feeling of oneness with mother is known as *bonding* or 'secure attachment', and is a very important factor in our later sense of well-being.

I have found that people who claim that they have intellectual problems with regard to faith in God are in fact generally rationalizing a pre-existing emotional problem of non-bonding, insecure attachment, or negative nurture at this early stage in their lives. I doubt very much if there is such a thing as a purely intellectual problem with regard to faith; firstly because of the nature of faith itself, and secondly because if there were genuine purely intellectual problems one would expect more intellectually gifted people to be faithless and less gifted people in this area to have deep faith. This in fact is not so.

The only relationship that I have consistently observed, between problems of faith and an individual's personality, is always emotional and in the realm of nurture. I would conclude by saying that this early stage of development is one in which the ability to deeply trust another person, or not to do so, is laid. Blessed indeed are those who have a good, or at least adequate, mother as a nurturer!

A very perceptive expression of how this stage of faith actually feels in the spiritual and emotional experience of the individual person can be found in Psalm 131, verses 3 and 4 (ASB Translation}

3. But I have calmed and quieted my soul
like a weaned child upon its mother's breast:
Like a child on its mother's breast
is my soul within me.
4. O Israel trust in the Lord;
from this time forward and forever.

Here the psalmist is appealing to the early experience of the mother-child symbiotic relationship as a model for faith in the here and now of adult experience. Unfortunately this can only have any validity for those whose relationship with mother at this stage of emotional development was either good, or at least adequate. We will look at the practical consequences of this later (Chapter 14) when the application of these insights will be considered.

5.4 Transitions between faith stages

Faith-stage progressions are not of the type A to B to C, and so on. Rather they are generally cumulative, A to AB to ABC etc. In other words, each new stage takes in components of each previous stage as a totality of faith identity is built up.

Between every stage of development there is a period of transition. Whether mindfully acknowledged or not, these tend to be painful times when the person outgrows the previous stage, but has not yet entered fully into the next one. People in transitions between stages are always particularly vulnerable, needing extra support until they pass through it. The symptoms of being in transition are an overwhelming feeling of loss: loss of faith, of happiness and of blessedness. Trust is threatened because the person wonders if they will ever be or feel up-together again, and all previous hurts seem to come back. There is a general feeling of returning to stage one, or even to non-existence in severe cases.

Teresa of Avila in her work 'The Interior Castle' (written in 1577) gives a graphic description of transition stages in the spiritual life that is well worth serious study. Many people also see the story of Adam and Eve being expelled from the Garden of Eden as a description of transition, especially of the transition from the innocence of infancy into the dangers and traumas of early childhood.

The first infant transition comes when baby grows too big for mother to hold and protect. It has thrust upon it an awareness of a larger, more complicated and less comfortable world into which it now has to enter and live. The pain of this is a tension between the excitement and urge to discover new things on the one hand, and the desire to cling to that which it knows already on the other. Growing baby cannot go backwards because she or he is too big, but to go forwards is uncomfortable and threatening because it demands adventure into the unknown. The movement ahead has two requirements. Firstly, that nurture in the previous stage was adequate, and secondly that functioning support structures are available to help the infant through its first transition stage since being born (which was of course a huge transition in itself).

These sorts of feelings come back again and again in adult life whenever a period of change or transition comes upon us. The feelings are always infantile, and how we cope with them goes way back to how we coped with our first transition from infant to toddler, and what emotionally-related resources were available to us at that time. Adequate resources at this early stage of our lives give us the trust we need to work through adult crises in the here and now as grown-ups. Inadequate resources during this early stage make us doubt and fear if we can find any similar adequate sources of help in adult crises now, and also tend to deprive us of the ability to use available resources appropriately.

Chapter 6

Stage 2 – An 'Intuitive-Projective' Faith

This second stage of James Fowler's sequence relates to the ages of two to five years, or thereabouts. It is the stage in our development in which we have enough autonomy to begin to be aware of, and discover, the world in which we live. Yet it is a stage in which the inner resources for doing this are limited. At this stage of life we do not have a very developed intellect. Our verbal and literal skills by which to interpret experience are few, though we do have a widening experience of the concrete realities in our environment.

The tools we do have at this 'toddler and beyond' stage of life, to use in our discovery and interpretation, are those of intuition and projection. By this time we also have a good enough range of emotions that give messages of: pleasant or unpleasant, good or bad, safe or dangerous. Therefore, we begin to construct from our experience at this phase a basic value system to do with what is trustworthy and what is not, that will tend to run through our whole life. The bases of our formative prejudices are also being firmed up at this stage.

6.1 Intuition

There are roughly three main ways in which the term 'intuition' is understood. They have a tendency more towards overlapping with each other or extending the scope of understanding, than they do of opposing each other.

The one understanding is that it is some kind of spiritual or magical 'knowing' by which people just know things to be so without having any empirical evidence for doing so. Many attribute this more to women than men. The term 'feminine intuition' is widely used and accepted as valid, on the grounds that women do seem in a large degree to have this sort of insight, especially within the context of relationships. I have observed this to be true also of some men, both in my own experience and also in an extensive study of biographies of great characters in history. One male example of this is Napoleon. He seemed to be able to know what the enemy was thinking of doing, and act accordingly to oppose it. He also looked for this quality in people whom he appointed to various commands in his army. Napoleon often asked the question regarding a person suggested to him as being a suitable subject for promotion to the rank of general: 'Does he have the ability to know what the enemy is about to do before he does it?'

The second understanding of intuition is one that comes basically from empirical observation. It is that in interactions with other people there are those, known as intuitive, who know things about other people simply because they have the skill to observe the other person and quickly process the observation at an unconscious level, thus giving the appearance of knowing something without any empirical evidence. I see this as not very adequate because it does not give any description of the unconscious process, and therefore just underscores the first understanding.

The third view is that put forward by Carl Jung, who pursued among other things an understanding of the human unconscious. His is much more sophisticated than the other two, but in short it can be said that he would see intuition as a human attribute, present in everyone, but more dominant in some people. It is basically an internal way in which people perceive the world in which they live, a kind of 'knowing mechanism' that enables human beings to collect and understand information that they need for their relationships and everyday living. A more complete understanding of this view of intuition can be obtained through, for example, study of the Myers-Briggs

Personality Types Indicator.

I believe that Jung's observations are basically correct; especially that intuition is not just a feminine attribute but that it is common to all human beings. I would add to this an observation that it appears to be more predominant in primitive peoples and the apparently less sophisticated. It would seem that in those people where intuition is weak, sophistication and rationalistic types of conditioning can crush it. Yet even in those societies that are rationalistic and sophisticated, those with strong intuitive tendencies, such as various kinds of artists and poets, do not lose this facility. They often become the prophetic element within that society.

6.2 Projection at Stage 2

We have already discussed human projection in Chapter 3. It is, in short, the ability to put onto other people, or objects, a number of situational feelings and emotions that essentially belong within us. At this second stage of faith this is done in combination with our intuitive 'knowing mechanism' as a means of testing out the environment in which we live, exploring it and discovering a satisfactory way of relating to it. Hence the Fowler term of the 'intuitive-projective' stage. Let us now look at some practical examples of how this works in a child at this stage of development.

Two examples observed

These are both from observations of my own (now adult) children at this stage of their development. I choose them because during this period of their life I had close and continual contact with them. The first example shows how the projections are made onto inanimate objects as a means of testing and discovery; and the second shows how accurate intuitive projections can be when directed towards other people.

i) Clocks with powers!

Between the age of 3 and 5 years I regularly took one of my sons with me on various trips. On one, to the bank in the local small town, I used to park in the square under the town clock, which was situated in its own tall slim tower. One day he said to me, 'Daddy, that is a Tini Clock.' 'Oh yes,' I said, 'tell me more about Tini Clock.' He then went on in great detail to explain that Tini Clock was a good and friendly clock whom he could trust because it was very tall and always looked down on him with a very kind face. I related this to the adult world in which he lived, of family and friends, because this period of our life was very stable and happy, and so he 'personified' the clock in this way. It is also easy to see how a child at this stage of development could project this sort of identity onto God.

As we traveled around, the next experience we had was when passing through a larger, strange town and he made a remark about another clock. This one was in the face of a large building, like a town hall, overlooking a busy central square. 'Daddy,' he said, 'that clock is a Miller.' At the time I was unable to say anything, other than to acknowledge what he had said, because I was very tense due to traffic density and being in a strange place. Later, however, we did talk about 'Millers' in detail. They were personified as always bad, untrustworthy, and to be avoided. I understood this to come from his emotional awareness. At the time 'Millers' were first encountered, the environmental situation was tense and not very pleasant. The feelings inside him were then projected onto a certain kind of clock as a means of coping with the emotions surrounding the situation and forming some manageable concept of evil. The same process had already taken place in the opposite way in projecting onto Tini Clock the feelings of security he was experiencing at the time.

Over the next year or two whenever we passed a clock I would ask him if it was a Tini Clock or a Miller. His reply was most interesting because very rarely were they either, but most often another kind of clock he called a 'Logit'. These were a neutral kind of clock, not very interesting, neither good nor bad. I came to realize that because he had no strong feelings, either pleasant or unpleasant, at the time, the concept of 'Logit' was totally consistent with all his intuitive projections and that he was in the process of building his own faith and evaluation system. This faith system was totally practical. An analogy of it could be that of an organism biologically adapting itself to its environment in order to survive and live.

In relational and spiritual terms, and at a very basic level, is this not what faith is about? Namely: Whom or what can I trust with the important issues in my life?

ii) Projected intuitions making contact with particular persons

We have looked at an example of intuitive projections put on to inanimate objects. Now I give two examples of such projections being placed onto particular people.

The first one is based on observation of another of my children when at this stage of development. As a mature adult he still retains the qualities of perception demonstrated as a child (the ABCD...progression), but does not remember the instances, which were frequent, of using his intuition in a projective way between the ages of three and five.

At the time I was vicar of a parish, and many people came to the vicarage to see me for a wide variety of reasons. This son went through a phase of answering the door to people, and nearly always got there first because his enthusiasm to do so was much greater than that of anyone else in the household! Having opened the door and invited the person in, he would then tell me exactly how he perceived them. For example, 'Daddy, there is a very happy man to see you,' or 'a miserable old man,' or a 'sad young lady,' or a 'nasty character,' and so on. I was aware that these simple and direct responses were almost always true. Very rarely did someone he said was sad turn out to be happy, or someone nasty, a nice person.

The second example of this is when I once looked after the child of a family in the parish because the parents had to go to hospital with his older brother. The child was four at the time. At one point we were working together in the garden when a woman walked in. Before telling me what she wanted, she attempted to talk in a kind of patronizing way to the child. The boy promptly turned his back on this woman and stared intently at the ground. She could get no response from him. After she had gone I asked him why he behaved as he did; his response was direct and unambiguous. 'She's horrible,' he said. I happened to get to know this woman well, subsequently, and the boy was correct in his intuitive-projective judgment, even though it was made with no other knowledge of the woman at the time.

I have had many other experiences of this kind with children of this age, and have come to believe that this is an expression of the intuitive-projective attribute by which they put out feelers towards others in order to find out if they can trust them. With inanimate objects the projections are of what is felt or experienced within the child. However, when projections are put onto living persons, then some kind of transmission comes back, thereby giving the child information to do with the nature of the other person.

6.3 Further reflections on the intuitive-projective stage

This important close-to-base stage of faith, if properly developed through the individual having a secure childhood within which this can be adequately worked out, enables an attitude towards the world and other people from which further fruitful developments of faith can grow. I also see it as being an important stage to which adults need to return regularly (from stages CDE etc…to B) as a contribution towards maintaining their own adult faith.

It has been well said that when we lose contact with the child we once were, we die. In order to do this with success we must have an adequately developed 'child' to which we can return without the fear and unbearable pain that an abused or hurt and neglected childhood prompts such people to retain. There are two statements made very firmly by Jesus Christ that are relevant here.

The first is in St. Matthew's Gospel 18:3, 4. Then He said:

> *I tell you solemnly, unless you change and become like a little child you will never enter the kingdom of heaven. And so, the one who makes himself as little as this little child is the greatest in the kingdom of heaven.*

It seems to me that this is a statement about the importance of the intuitive-projective stage; not only that it should be adequately worked through at the appropriate chronological age, but that something from it is an important factor for every stage and age of our lives. This idea will be further developed later.

The second relevant Jesus saying is in the same chapter of St. Matthew's Gospel verses 5 to 7:

> *Anyone who welcomes a child like this in my name welcomes me. But anyone who is an obstacle to bring down one of these little ones who have faith in me would be better drowned in the depths of the sea with a great millstone round his neck. Alas for the world that there should be such obstacles! Obstacles indeed there must be, but alas for the man who provides them!*

This is quoted merely to demonstrate the importance of this stage in the development of faith.

Both this one, and the previous saying, lay foundations upon which later developments in faith can take place. It seems that without this kind of formation, faith cannot grow in a person at a later stage in life. It would also be true to say that many of our so called adult and intellectual crises of faith have roots in this stage of our lives. For any resolution of these crises we must track back stage-wise, as I intend to do later when considering the various pastoral and spiritual implications of these stages in our development.

My second reflection here is that as we grow older and further away from the intuitive projective stage we seem to want to destroy it or deny it. We use terms like 'irrational' when we have a strong 'hunch' about something, and deny its validity as a means of knowing, because we accept a biased educational conditioning that says that only the rational is valid. Of course this Fowler stage is irrational in the strictest sense of the word, because it is *pre*-rational. I think that this tendency to deny has two roots.

The first is a result of our culture following that period of Western history called 'The Enlightenment' or the 'Age of Reason'. It seems to me that during that phase of cultural history the baby was literally thrown away with the bath water, and that many activities today broadly associated with 'New Age' and 'alternative' therapies are reactions aimed at recovering a better balance. As counter reactive movements they are sometimes not very balanced, and can lead to an anti-rationalism which is as bad as the rationalists' denial of the irrational.

The other root of the adult tendency to deny child-like thoughts is I think more practical. As we enter the next stages of any process we need to deny, or at least not give much heed to the agenda of the previous stage. Then we feel freer to enter and explore the stage we are now at, with all that it demands of us. A child who is at school is very upset and resentful at being considered a baby. They have to become a big boy or girl and do need encouraging in moving on.

It is true that under stress some degree of regression always takes place, but this is painful for a young person to admit, and it is only in quite mature adulthood that we can admit easily to any form of regressive behavior. I would say then that it is normal for anyone in the next one or two stages of their development to deny attributes from an earlier stage. However, when one has moved a few stages further on, then it is both normal and healthy to go back and take up again what has been the agenda of a previous stage at an appropriate time and in an appropriate situation. We will take up this issue again a few more stages on when the appropriateness of doing so will become more evident (see Chapter 11).

The third matter of note at this pre-rational stage is that 'vibes' or transmissions, from persons are a very important factor in both knowing and communicating. As I demonstrated earlier, small children just know by this means if they are loved, and they thrive and grow when they are. This links us as human beings with aspects of the animal world.

Animals do not have word language, and if they have intellect it is not developed as in a human being. My father, who was a farmer, used to say that if one wanted to test the suitability of a person to look after cows, one should take that person for a walk among them and observe how they react. It is also a fact that cows will always give much more milk when a person to whom they relate well milks them. This principle is true of all animals; they know those things that are essential for their well-being, and they do so without the aid of rational processes that lead to achieving skills such as language and literacy.

Isaiah, the prophet, in the following statement bewails the fact that Israel has lost this basic attribute that animals do not lose:

> The ox knows its owner
> and the ass its master's crib;
> Israel knows nothing,
> My people understands nothing'
> (Isaiah 1:3)

6.4 The next transition

The period of transition to the next stage of faith comes with the development of intellect and the growth of language that runs alongside. This gives us the ability to differentiate, and to define and further understand that which we are experiencing. This thus adds another dimension to what we already have, and when this happens there is always confusion about the validity of what went before. The earlier stage can be seen as redundant, and of no further use, hence some of the roots of denial.

However, it is only when we are much further along the developmental road that we able integrate that which is valid from the past into our present faith system. As soon as we have entered our new state of being with its new and exciting skills, it is obvious that we need to put the past behind us for a while and to explore our new horizons. One-track mindedness is the only possible lifestyle, at least for the time being.

Chapter 7

Stage 3 – The 'Mythic Literal' Phase of Faith

The one track along which the young person runs at this third stage of faith is that of reducing everything to being good or bad, right or wrong. This is a very 'black and white' stage. The main reason for this is because the newly acquired power of intellect is one that serves to define experiences, to put them into categories so that they can be understood and handled. The external world that is now being experienced is very large and frightening. Hence to adopt a black and white approach of defining and understanding gives a degree of security that makes a person feel safe, so enabling a person to 'learn one's way around' this ever increasing world of experiences. This is what is meant by 'literal' and is the dominant factor of this stage.

The mythic aspect of this stage refers to the medium through which the person's experience is enlarged and their personal experiences tested. It is simply through the use of story. For a youngster around this stage of development, story-telling is of vital importance. They have the ability to become totally absorbed in a story, and then, when at play, to act it out. The acting out is a kind of practice dry run for confronting the issues with which they will have to deal in adult life. The story provides the stimulus and means for this to happen. Children who cannot partake in this story-telling and living out through play are handicapped, both faithwise, and in their ability to cope emotionally when they become adults. Let us now develop this opening statement in more detail.

7.1 The mythic dimension

Mythology is a very important aspect of human understanding, and remains so throughout our life even though it originates and is dominant in our understanding at this stage of development. The word 'myth' in present times has been made to be synonymous with false. This has been caused, I believe, by the popularity of what I would call pseudo-science, a belief based upon an inadequate understanding of science, which holds blindly that the scientific method can, by careful application to all areas of our experience, give us accurate understanding that differentiates between truth and falsehood. This view is in itself an attitude of faith based upon a mythology. The scientific method, in common with any other method of understanding, needs to have its own mythology in order that it might develop and function. Why is this so? Simply because all knowledge is partial, and knowledge obtained by means of the scientific method is no different in this respect from any other form of knowledge. All knowledge is in reality dependent upon the instruments by which the knowledge is obtained, and those instruments are always in the last resort subject to human judgment. I would suggest that the popular denial that the scientific method has its own mythologies, and indeed needs them, might well be to do with its comparative newness in our development as human beings. Therefore, as already pointed out, there is a need and pressure to deny what has gone before so that the new experience can be fully explored.

Let us now define what is meant by myth so that what has already been said can be explored in more detail. I would define a myth as 'a story that is the vehicle for containing and communicating a profound truth'. Such forms the basis of a belief system on which we depend to give our life meaning and purpose. Without myths we cannot live; they are an integral part of being human. There are two reasons for this. The first is that our mythologies give us an identity and sense of well-being for the here and now of living; and secondly, they provide us with the means of developing and moving forward as human beings.

I would claim that the first kind of myth is generally about how spiritually, sociologically, and psychologically based mythologies originate and function, and that the second kind are ones at the basis of scientific mythologies.

Two other important issues on the subject of myths and mythologies are that they can be either true or false. It is often the case that a mythology that served well, and was 'true' for one stage of our development, can become false at a later stage simply because we have moved on. Also there are some myths which have an abiding quality and are eternally true, whereas those that are temporary, in that they only relate to a certain specific stage of development, need to be cast aside and new ones created to replace them. Mythologies, therefore, are not static. They are living and changing phenomena. Old ones die and are rejected, new ones are continually being created. In this manner they are very much an integral part of faith, its expression and outworking in our everyday lives.

My task now is to give some examples of the different types of myth and look at how they develop, together with the purpose they serve. The four categories mentioned above will be considered separately and their relationship to each other, as well as to other factors, will be considered.

7.2 Spiritual mythology

To illustrate this I will use the Bible, and do so from a Christian point of view, because as a Christian myself I have an understanding and familiarity with it that will enable me to express more adequately what I want to say.

The Bible is not in fact one book but a large collection of books written and put together over a period of several thousand years. The authors of the books, some known, others not known, are all very different people. However, there are several common themes to do with the big issues of human life that run through it all and are in tune with life as we live it today. Some books are history, others poetry, some are mythology and some are a mixture of all three. For Christians, the focus and central point of this great library of spiritual history and interpretation is the very historical person, Jesus Christ. This includes some understanding of who he is, which we get in writings that give us the spiritual experiences and reflections of those who were close to him during his lifetime, and in the years just after this time.

It is very evident that in the Christian Tradition the whole of the Bible is interpreted through the eyes of Jesus Christ, who was born and bred as a Jew. What is equally true is that Jesus himself was a part of the greater tradition that is contained in the whole Bible and its ancillary literature. In this tradition mythology plays a great part because it is used as a vehicle for truths and spiritual experiences that transcend simple human logic. As such they cannot be contained or transmitted by means of simple statements, dogmas, formulas or rules, so beloved by us human beings. The message is too big and important for this kind of simplistic reductionism.

Jesus Christ taught in the main through the means of parable and story. We are told that he did so because:

> They may see and see again, but not perceive; may hear, and hear again, and not understand; otherwise they might be converted and be forgiven.
> St. Mark, Chapter 4

This explanation by Jesus is not original. It is in the tradition of the Bible and appears also in the Old Testament, in chapter 6 of Isaiah. In both cases its purpose seems to be to hold people back from understanding and being healed or converted. I have experienced many people raging about this because they would like it all made simple, and the Bible makes it hard. Likewise, mythology has a kind of parabolic mystery. Although parable and myth are not the same thing, they do have this in common:

they force people to wrestle with and agonize over certain aspects of deep spiritual truth, never giving a simple well-defined answer. Both would appear to push people away from belief.

I believe that this is so for two reasons. Firstly, that understanding spiritual truths is dependent upon faith, and where a person is in the development of their faith. Secondly, that if spiritual truth is handed out simply, as if it were on a plate, it would be misunderstood and corrupted by those not yet ready to receive it. Therefore it must come after a preparatory process of spiritual wrestling; there is no other way. *Religious ideas which people have that they receive solely by means of informing the intellect are all inadequate* and often subtly false. The love of God as expressed through Jesus could not allow this because we must have a faith and understanding that is relevant to where we are in life in terms of faith development.

Religious mythology serves to supply this. It is there, containing always the gold of deep spiritual truth, but we have to wrestle to mine and refine it for ourselves at each stage of our development. Those things in mythology that are not relevant for us at any given time can be ignored or walked away from, but they will still be there for us when we are ready to return to them.

The mythic awareness that comes at this third stage of faith is an asset that we have for the whole of our lives. It should be seen as a tool to be used appropriately for the rest of our lives, and also an indication of the eternal and lasting quality of those deeper truths that are contained in what I describe as 'spiritual mythology'. We have looked at the relationship between mythology and parable in the spiritual dimension. This does show us how it is hard to draw rigid boundaries between what is myth and what is not. The same is true of history. It is a known fact that ancient historians put words into the mouths of important historical people. This does not invalidate those words spiritually because they are in a sense a mythology that gives expression to the spirit of that person, and in such terms could be most accurate if they come from the pen of one who really knew the historic person, and had a deep personal relationship with them. I think that this applies to some of the New Testament writings about Jesus Christ.

There are, however, stories in the Bible that could be pure mythology, such as the Book of Ruth and the Book of Jonah. To get the spiritual message of such texts, which is eternally true, one should read them thoughtfully and let them speak to the soul. It is quite pointless, for example, to debate whether or not it is possible for Jonah to have stayed alive in the stomach of a fish for three days and nights. This is a very immature attitude, and having said this leads us on naturally to a discussion of the literal aspect of 'mythic literal' stage. But before doing this we must look at other kinds of mythology.

7.3 Sociological mythology

These are the mythologies which enshrine the values of the society in which we grew up and were nurtured. They are primarily cultural but can also be politicized.

By the word 'culture' I mean that set of values, attitudes and, to us, essentially self-evident 'truths' that surround us, being taken for granted, and used as a kind of shorthand for communication. An example is, 'British is Best'; therefore every product with 'British Made' stamped on it must always be superior. Another example: at parties, in pubs and clubs, or wherever people meet to relax and exchange yarns, stories are told about how unreliable foreign cars are, or about the foreign-made saucepan whose handle just fell off, whereas British-made saucepans are known of which last three generations and are still as good as new! Thus when such stories are told they reinforce the mythology of the belief that 'British Made' equals superior quality. This of course may or may not be true. Such can be a genuine expression of loyalty to one's own country that is healthy, or it can be the basis of extreme right-wing political dogmas that are both false and repugnant. Historical fact does have a part in these mythologies, in that there once could have been a time when British-made products were in certain, even many, fields superior to all others, but they may not still be so. The need to hold onto this mythology could be that British goods are no longer best, and this so threatens the national identity that a move to politicize it comes from a deeply felt gut reaction of insecurity which brings about a need to strengthen a sense of national identity. Such is the basis of appeal of political movements like the National Front.

In Germany in the last century the Nazi mythology of the super-race surrounding WWII grew out of a need to restore the morale and sense of identity of a WWI-defeated nation that felt itself to be unjustly treated and had to prove its own value. There are many other examples of social and political mythologies being created by nations, tribes, and groups of people in order to give the individuals within them a sense of pride, well-being and identity, or to restore what they feel is being lost when that which is being lost is of great value culturally to individuals within any particular nation group or society. Other examples of this are: Plaid Cymru and the Welsh Language Society; the Scottish National Party; the movement for a greater Serbia based on the mythology surrounding the battle of Kosovo in which the Serbs believed themselves to have been sacrificed in order to preserve Europe from an Islamic onslaught; and so on. Indeed, examples are innumerable.

I cite them as examples of how tribal and nationalistic mythologies develop and become perpetuated, but there are also ones that enshrine group political ideas so that groups of people can be motivated to achieve certain goals. A particular example of this is Marxism. It is a mythology that enshrines a belief that all the evils of this world are caused by a minority of people having all the money, and with it power; whereas the majority, because they do not have the money and power, are vulnerable and exploited in an unjust way. The answer to this is the creation of a just society by overthrowing those who control and exploit, and then letting the exploited share the wealth out more equally according to need. In this mythology there are goodies in conflict with baddies. Those who are believers in the message the mythology enshrines would expect the goodies to win, because what they see as 'moral right' is on their side. Again, one could cite many other political mythologies to demonstrate the same point, but I use this as an example only in an argument and not in any way as a complete exposition of Marxism.

The points I wish to make in citing very briefly all the above examples are: firstly, that sociological mythologies all arise out of a combination of human need that relates directly to historical situations. Secondly, they also serve a very valuable purpose in both giving individuals a sense of identity and value, and also in motivating them to take action aimed at solving problems. Thirdly, they all contain truths, but also quite often can become redundant and even false as time moves on. This is where they differ from spiritual mythologies that tend towards enshrining more transcendental and eternal truths.

Finally, I wish to point out a danger inherent in all sociological mythologies. This is that they are more potent in an age of mass communication. Mass media can use such mythologies in ways that misinform. This is because a quickly flashed image on a TV screen can trigger off many deeply ingrained sociological mythologies in those who watch, which are so widely different from each other; the end result being that each viewer becomes merely reinforced in his or her own cultural prejudices rather than being informed. But the belief system enshrined in media mythology is that what is being offered to the viewer is 'mere information'.

The negative nature of much sociological mythology can be seen in this example. It has great power to be divisive and also destructive of wider human understanding and tolerance. It can also deceive in very subtle ways. Modern means of mass communication are a very powerful tool for creating modern sociological mythologies, which can be either good or evil, depending upon the morality of those who control those media. The advertising industry is one that trades on this by using and manipulating the mythologies that already exist in the minds of viewers and listeners, and also in common with other aspects of the media, creating new ones that may either be true or false, good or evil.

7.4 Psychological mythologies

As a means of demonstrating what I mean by psychological mythologies I intend to use the theories of Eric Berne, which he used in his method of demonstrating how people relate to each other, called *Transactional Analysis*. I find this a very useful tool because it is simple and has a very obvious relationship to what we actually experience in our daily lives. Berne's intention was to help people inter-relate better by giving them a model that would show the origins of emotions and attitudes that are experienced when in relationship with other people during adulthood.

Berne's theory states that in everyone there are '*three centers of awareness*'. These are, firstly, *The Child Center*, which consists of all the emotions and attitudes that originate from when we were a small child, and are still active within us. Secondly, *The Parent Center*, which consists of all the emotions and attitudes that were internalized by us from the adult world in which we were nurtured. This second center of awareness is largely imposed upon us from outside, whereas the child center of awareness comes mainly from within, being a more accurate indication of what we really are like in our basic nature. The third one is *The Adult Center*, which has a rational basis and grows within us as we become adult.

When considering how our psychological mythologies develop it is the *Parent Center of Awareness* that is most important, because it is this one that comes into being during the mythic-literal stage of faith development and enables psychological mythologies to be developed. In relationship to this the term 'scripting' is also of importance. It is used to describe values, and patterns of behavior that are 'written in' to a child's personality at this stage of development. These become so ingrained that they usually persist for the rest of a person's life. It is possible to change them, but this is not easy or always necessary, unless they become negative and damaging by preventing people from becoming sufficiently themselves in adulthood. I see psychological mythologies as being a vehicle for containing these scripts. Often they are elaborate, and they reinforce the belief systems of the scripts, giving them power.

Next I give some examples of psychological mythologies. In principle all these mythologies are stories that enshrine and reinforce certain beliefs and attitudes. These are told and retold in families, at schools on speech days and on other occasions as a means of strengthening the resolve of the young and giving them direction in life. As an example of a family psychological mythology, let us take a family in which the value system is that one works hard to make money, is never beholden to anyone, pays one's way in the world and also gives money to charity for the support of a class of people who are poor because they are inferior. In such a family, stories would be told of heroes in the family such as the uncle who left school at fourteen, started as the office boy in a firm that sold tea, rose to be a manager, then a director and ended up founding the biggest supermarket chain in the country. In support of this older members of the family would say to their young such things as: 'I remember Lord X when he pushed a barrow in London's East End,' or, 'The firm that makes these pills, now having hundreds of branches, was started by a woman who traveled the world looking for herbs and working to pay her way, doing any job that she could get to earn the money. Now the firm she founded supports a number of charities for supplying medicines to the third world poor.'

Such rags to riches mythologies, with a touch of human charitableness in them, are internalized by children and form their attitudes to the world in which they live. This could be good if the child is a person with the right natural gifts to use them as motivation for their own fulfillment. However, if a child in such a family does not have these natural endowments, but may be gifted as an artist, musician, or academically, then such mythology can do psychological damage, making them feel inferior or inadequate; the negative side being that poor people are inferior and that people gifted in such ways will tend to remain poor, or relatively poor, all their lives.

This example could be transferred in principle to every family, but each one would have different values and heroes that embodied them: they would also have anti-heroes. A poor family in a deprived area would have a mythology that would be the reverse of the one given as an example, and a musical or artistic family would have their own variation. All children at this stage of development will be deeply affected by these mythologies, some for good, and some for ill. As we shall see later, it is possible to moderate or change them, but only at the right stage of development.

Schools also have such mythologies, and the principles are the same. Examples of this are what is said in assemblies or on speech days. The characteristics of outside speakers invited in are an indication of the kind of mythologies a school wishes to build. The current practice in schools and other institutions of preparing mission statements is also a form of mythology building, which I would see as being both sociological and psychological. All this is clearly indicative of the stage of development of those for whom schools are primarily designed.

7.5 Scientific mythologies

I deliberately chose this classification for some mythologies because there is a wide misunderstanding of what science is about, and that it is to do with simple facts, and therefore does not need a mythology. I believe that not only does science have its own mythologies, but that it needs them for its own development. This is the case because the universe it seeks to explore is so vast that it cannot be understood without the use of mythology. Mythology is a basic human need and will always remain so. Human beings who study science need it because they are human. Those who are not scientists need it so that they can have a working understanding of their scientific fellows. One indisputable fact about science is that it is not static, but always changing. As more discoveries are made, so its theories about reality change in order that the new discoveries can be incorporated into the whole. Science is in essence a mode of discovery, not an ultimate truth in itself. Because it is a method it needs mythologies to enshrine the truths about where it now is on its path of discovery, so that it can move on from an accepted and understood basis.

An example of this is what is widely known as the theory of evolution. I see this as pure mythology because, firstly, the evidence to prove it conclusively has not yet been found; and, secondly, that such evidence that there is could possibly point in the direction of demonstrating that creation originated in this way rather than as a one-off or short series of acts. The strength of this mythology is that it does motivate some people to search for old bones that could be the missing link. For this reason alone it can be seen to bear the hallmarks of mythology. If all the required evidence were to be found, then the mythology would no longer be needed.

Scientific mythologies share with sociological mythologies this transient nature, whereas spiritual ones do not, because they enshrine truths that are of a totally different kind. Therefore to see a fundamental conflict between the Creation story in the book of Genesis and the scientific myth of evolution is to totally miss the point. Both are mythologies but they enshrine different 'truths' for different reasons.

By now enough has been said about the meaning of the word 'mythic' for us to understand what it is and set it within the context of the whole. The following are the main points of importance:

i) Mythology is a very important aspect of being human. It has a number of functions that are universal; without them we cease to be able to be fully human.
ii) Mythology's main function is to be a vehicle for containing and communicating certain truths about life that are too deep and complex to be expressed in simple prose or formulae.
iii) Mythology is an essential aspect of faith because it has the power to motivate and give us direction in our life's journey, whatever form or direction that journey might take for any individual person at any period of his or her life.
iv) An ability to create, understand and use mythology comes to us as human beings at the stage in childhood when intellect begins to develop, and our exposure to the adult world in which we are being nurtured is at its most sensitive and aware. This is the same stage at which our 'parent center of awareness' is being developed.
v) This stage is a cardinal one in human development. Together with the intuitive-projective stage out of which it finally develops with the growth of intellect, it is the most important and continuing aspect for us. It forms the foundation upon which all other understanding is based, and, as we shall see in later stages of faith development, it is one to which we continually return. If this foundation is sound, then all that develops from it will be sound. Little wonder that there is a saying attributed to the

> Jesuits: 'Give us a child until he or she is seven, and then do what you will'.

Finally, Jesus Christ himself was insistent that not only should we become 'like a little child' to enter into the kingdom of heaven, but also one of the gravest offences that an adult can commit is to destroy the faith of such a child who naturally believes in Him. I think that this indicates how crucial it is for the whole of our lives, faithwise, that this stage of development should be soundly nurtured. If it is not, a person can become a spiritual cripple for life, and unfortunately in my experience, many do.

7.6 The 'literal' aspect of this stage of faith

Compared with defining and elaborating 'mythic', very little needs saying about 'literal', for it is easily observed that children at this stage of maturing are very 'cut and dried' in their approach to life. All that they experience is judged easily as being good or bad, right or wrong, true or false. No clear distinction is made between the world of mythology and the world of objective reality. All their concepts are definite and concrete, with no grey areas, and abstract thinking is yet to emerge.

There are three important factors to consider in all this. The first one is that the 'literal' activity is purely rational. It comes from the growth for the first time of an awareness of intellect. This capacity to think as an independent person gives the individual power to control and organize experiences. Because at this stage these experiences are getting bigger and bigger with the threat of getting out of control, the intellect reduces them to a size that is manageable and non-threatening. Hence these youngsters create mythologies so as to contain their understanding of these experiences, tending to perceive experience and mythology as the same thing.

The second point arises directly out of the first one. It is that the use of the intellect, as described above, acts as a brake upon runaway mythologies and experiences that are emotionally disturbing. So here we would seem to have the origins of the use of intellect in the process of rationalization so widely used in adulthood, and which is at the root of all kinds of fundamentalism.

Thirdly, as the intellectual capacity develops it leads on to a transition stage. This is a crucial transition because it is the one that brings us from childhood into adulthood. All the foundations are now laid; all the equipment needed for our full humanity has been given; the big wide world of new experiences waits to be entered into and discovered. How positively and creatively this discovery is depends upon how these already given faculties are used; and also, if impaired or inadequately developed, how they will restrict the ability of a person to enter fully into life. Because the ending of this stage is pivotal in the whole development of faith, I intend at this point to end the foundations section with a conclusion that draws together the key factors we have looked at so far. All of them will be taken on into the next stages of adult development of faith and integrated, well or badly, into successive stages.

7.7 Interim review: Drawing together key issues so far discussed

There are five attributes laid down in childhood that are used as tools of perception and understanding as we develop our faith into adulthood. The stages of development from adolescence onward are not ones in which new attributes are gained, but ones in which those we already have from childhood are used and tuned more finely to deal with the things we experience as our world becomes more complex and demanding. I next define these five attributes, packaging them in a way suitable for them to be taken with us on our adult journey.

i) **The Undifferentiated Stage:** This is in practice a mystical sense of well-being and union with the source of our being. It is given to us (or not) in our early state of infancy through the experience we have with our mother, *(see Psalm 131)*, but as we shall see later it is experienced again in the more advanced stages of faith among the contemplatives and mystics. Many people also experience this from time to time at various stages of their life and faith development. This shows that the stages spelt out here are not rigid states but fluid ones. Some regression from a more advanced to a primitive stage and then back again is a frequent and not always unhealthy experience. The deep problem with this is when a person has a bad or inadequate nurture as an infant it means that they do not have anywhere into which they can regress and so experience the renewing power of trust in a loving source of being.

ii) **Intuitiveness:** When Carl Jung was asked if he believed in God, he replied, 'No, I do not; I know Him.' This was an intuitive response based upon personal experience. The question was put in terms that indicated its basis was intellectual and theoretical. It was based on theories about God, but Jung's reply was based upon experience of God. This shows how both intellect and intuition differ. Both are attributes of human personality with specific functions. Intuition is more about knowing through the means of relationships, i.e. 'whether we know we are loved, and can another person be trusted?' Since intellect is about analyzing and controlling information of all kinds, on their own *I doubt if our intellects are capable of acquiring real knowledge of other people or personal beings*. In our modern society intuition has been demeaned as a tool in the process of knowing, whereas intellect has been over-valued. Both are tools given to us for the purpose of knowing. We need therefore to use both as appropriate and carry them together in our tool-kit for life.

iii) **Projection:** This is a psychological mechanism we all have that 'puts out probes'. When we use projection in a way that blocks off receiving anything back, it is sick and destructive, because by so doing we are totally self-centered, and limit or even destroy our ability to relate to other persons. However, when we project a feeling or idea onto another person and receive a response back from them that makes us reconsider the content of our projection, and modify it, then we are using this attribute creatively. Healthy projection is an essential tool for forming and sustaining relationships, and thus also of continuing importance in faith development.

iv) **The mythological:** Without our mythologies we cannot live a life that is meaningful. We need them as vehicles to contain everything that gives us identity and purpose, for within the context of the universe we are so small, and our lives so complex that naked reality threatens to a point of near destruction. T.S. Elliot said, 'man cannot cope with too much reality.' We therefore are given the capacity to create mythologies so that through them we can ration reality to amounts with which we can cope. While it is essential that we make contact with the greater objective realities within the world around us, we can only do so by reducing their essence to manageable forms.

v) **Intellect:** Fowler uses the term *literal* in the last stage of childhood faith development, but I use the term intellect to describe that 'given' which we take with us into adulthood because the ability to make literal is pure intellectual activity. It is at this later stage, after all the other attributes are given, that intellect develops. It gives us the ability to form our mythologies from the material we already have through our experiences, and it also gives us the ability to evaluate and reform them. It does not on its own give us knowledge and understanding, but it is an essential factor in the process of gaining those. It is also a kind of safety mechanism, or brake, which stops our emotional responses to our experiences from running away with us. It is also a block that is put on our anxieties and fears. If used negatively it can destroy growth and creativity. On its own intellect is sterile, but without it creativity can get out of hand and become destructive. We will see the tension, or dialogue between intellect and the other attributes being continually worked out as we examine the following stages of faith development throughout adulthood. One example of intellect being used as a brake against fear is with respect to fundamentalism of all kinds – religious, scientific, social, and political. As we shall see, fundamentalism always blocks growth in faith and of developments in healthy relationships. Fundamentalism, sadly, is largely regressive for faith development that too many become stuck with.

7.8 An exercise

To end this section on childhood faith development I invite you, the reader, to do an exercise that has the purpose of testing out what has been said by applying it to yourself. It is simply to write down your own personal mythology as a means of stating who you perceive yourself to be now. Those who find this helpful could continue this practice by journal writing. This will show over a period of time how our mythologies need to change because they become outgrown, just as in physical terms we outgrow our clothes.

In writing your mythology, consider these aspects:

- i) In what situations do I feel relaxed, and at peace?
- ii) What would be my perfect job, house, partner, status in life, place to live?
- iii) What do I perceive as being evil, and also good?
- iv) Within what kinds of situations do I feel uncomfortable, or disturbed?

Attempt to relate your answers to all these questions to your childhood history and to actual objective events, both in the past and in the present. Try to be aware of how you gathered the information: that is, from feelings you have but do not understand; and from intuitions or projections received, but not reflected upon.

Finally, note that this material is all very personal to you. Hence what you do with it is entirely your responsibility, but it could be very helpful to share and discuss your material with someone whom you trust and who knows you well.

Chapter 8

Stage 4 – The Synthetic-Conventional Adult Phase

We now reach the point at which we begin to consider how faith grows, matures and develops during adulthood. The stage in our lives, known as adolescence, can be aptly described as a fresh 'period of birth' from childhood into adulthood.

As we have just seen, in terms of faith development, all the gifts and attributes laid down during childhood give us the equipment we need for our faith journey in adulthood. This can be seen as a spiritual and emotional reflection of what happened during our physical birth. We were contained in our mother's womb until we were developed enough physically to be able to live outside it, then came the time of thrusting out from the womb in the process called 'birth'. In faith development the protected environment of childhood can be seen as 'a womb of the spirit' in which we develop that which we need to live an adult life of faith. Then, during adolescence, we are born into the adult faith world and have certain tasks to perform so that we can gain a faith autonomy which will serve us for the journey ahead. It is the gaining of this faith autonomy that we will now explore. Fowler calls this fourth stage the 'synthetic- conventional'.

The main agenda of this stage of faith can be summed up in one word, *Sabaoth*. This is a Hebrew word and it appears in the first known Christian hymn, the *Te Deum*. In this hymn God is praised because He is the Lord God of Sabaoth. In modern parlance I would translate this as meaning, *God you are great because you can get your act together* – a very adolescent sentiment that contains a large amount of projected desire! The adolescent is very concerned with getting his or her 'act together' and being their true self.

The two aspects of projection and prejudice, which we have already discussed as being important factors in faith, are very evident at this stage of its development. As we shall see later, there are two arenas in which both of these play a great part during adolescence. They are the dogmatic and at times irrational authority given to the peer group, and the equally dogmatic and irrational way in which projections are made onto authority figures, hero figures and role models, in both negative and positive ways.

It is during this outworking of prejudice and projection that, little by little, the adolescent gets his or her act together. They marshal the resources they already have from childhood so that they can put together a synthesis of these things that can be validated by the group in which their day-to-day life is being lived out. This is what synthetic-conventional means in brief. Now we shall explore it in more detail, subdividing the issues under five headings for convenience.

8.1 Human will

The noun 'will' is often used in association with the word 'power'. People are often exhorted to use their 'will-power' in order to overcome problems, resist temptations or achieve goals. Weak-willed people are seen as failures, unreliable, and usually despised. Translated into terms of faith, the strong-willed are seen as being faithful, and the weak-willed as being faithless. Therefore we now raise the questions of what is meant by will, of how it relates to faith and of how it is acquired.

The short answer to this last question is: By projecting our prejudices that are already formed onto external objects, mostly people, and then formulating a set of beliefs on how we understand the nature of the response we get. Again, when this process is reduced to the simplest form, there are three categories of value to be considered. Where there is no response, then there is nothing of worth out there; where the response is positive, then it must be fully considered; and finally, where it is negative it must be rejected as being bad. Here we become aware of the relationship between faith and morality, as recent studies, by for example Leslie Francis, have shown. We will therefore examine moral development later, but for the time being we concentrate upon faith development.

Those who have dealings with adolescents know the power of their will. Parents are often engaged in a kind of constant warfare, as are those who run organizations such as youth clubs. The sense can be of warfare, but adults must always be alert to possible strong projections. I experienced this both as a parent and also as a youth club leader. Some twenty years later I am aware of the results of how I responded to these projections when my own adult children and those who were in youth clubs told me about how they now felt and what they believed. I now give two illustrations.

Between the ages of about 30 and 47, I was involved almost continually in running youth clubs in villages. Towards the end of this time, when exhaustion was setting in, I sought to hand over to others. I had working with me at the time a local farmer whom I would describe as a mature and balanced caring man with a solid practical faith. Like myself, he felt the exhaustion of years of this 'warfare', and so we looked for a younger person to take over from both of us. At the time an outgoing and energetic young man who had recently come to live in the village was suggested. When approached he was extremely keen to take over. I gathered that he would improve everything and bring it all up to date. So he took over with an air of great confidence, stating that the club would become the best the village had ever known. We, the old management, were greatly relieved, but our peaceful retirement lasted only a few months. I had pleas from the young people for myself and the farmer to come back because everything was falling to pieces. I also had a visit from the young man who wanted to give it all up on the grounds that the youth were totally uncooperative and undermined all he attempted to do.

On reflection, what was going on in this situation? It seems to me that the younger man was not mature enough to handle all the projections that the young people were putting upon him, because he was, albeit unwittingly, using the club as an arena in which to work out his own agenda. This meant that the young people could not get back the kind of response from him that they needed for their development. His leadership, though well-intended, triggered negative vibes in the youth club members and had to be rejected. The farmer and I gave positive response because, although exhausted, we were mature enough not to be over bothered by what they thought of us. We both had unflattering nicknames, and as a result created a stable environment in which they felt safe to work out their own agendas.

My second illustration comes from a recent conversation with my 34 year old son. He said that the best thing I did for him as an adolescent was to spend time in argument with him so that the point at issue was always worked through to some sort of satisfactory conclusion. I recall these occasions as being times of great exhaustion during which I just had the energy to hang in. But now I am glad I did, and attribute my doing so to the fact that I loved him, cared about the truth, and was mature enough not to be using him to work out my own inadequacies.

The place of *will* in such processes is essential. The young person must have enough will power to assert the projections. Those upon whom the projections are being placed must have the will to be able to accept them, hold them and allow the response to be of a positive nature. Holding the projection does not mean accepting it as valid, let alone taking it personally. Rather the very holding of the projection for long enough in dialogue enables the person making it to work out its value.

Rollo May defines *will* as: 'The capacity to organize oneself so that movement in a certain direction or toward a certain goal may take place.' I find this remarkably biblical, in line with what I have already said about the word *Sabaoth*. As the Bible is primarily about faith one should not be surprised at this. Sadly, only too often the Bible is not properly understood, and as a result greatly misused. May also examines the psychological roots of will that he sees as 'wish'. By the use of imagination people, especially adolescents, build up fantasies about what should be, or could be, in their lives. These fantasy wishes are then tried out by projecting them onto other people, getting, hopefully, an honest response. Ultimately this process leads to the strengthening of the will to move on positively in life. This indicates that for positive and reliable faith to develop, a healthy will is essential. For both of these the right environment must be provided. Again, what May says brings to mind the *Spiritual Exercises of Ignatius Loyola* (see bibliography) as a means of faith development. Their basis is in the use of imagination as a means of understanding scripture and developing personal faith. These also emphasize having the correct structure or support system within which the individual does the exercises. Both of these factors point towards its relevance for the synthetic-conventional stage of faith development.

The title of May's book, from which I have quoted a definition of will, is '*Love and Will*'. I think this is significant, for love defines the nature of the support structure in which a healthy will can be developed. What I have said about the Bible applies equally to love. That also has often been misunderstood, mainly I believe because it is complicated and one has to grow and develop to a certain level of maturity before it can be a means of support for someone at the stage of development, faithwise or emotionally, that is now being described. I would say that the two examples from my own experience demonstrate this, especially that of the younger man whom the youth club rejected. The cause of the rejection was that they did not feel safe with him, and therefore could not work out their own agenda needs under his leadership. May indicates this when he attributes the many problems of modern society in relationships to people lacking the will to cope:

> 'Anxiety is rampant, we cling to each other and try to persuade ourselves that what we feel is love; we do not 'will' because we are afraid that if we choose one thing or one person we'll lose the other, and we are too insecure to take that chance.'

This indicates very accurately the most important fact of this faith stage. It is that it is very transient, and cannot be worked through to the maturity of a later one unless those who have matured well beyond it are present to provide facilitating support structures. The most essential attribute to be gained at this developmental stage is the will to move on, hence the space devoted to this subject.

8.2 Three governing factors of this stage of faith

a) *The two-way look*

Like the Roman God Janus, after whom the month January is named, the adolescent, and all who are at this stage of faith, look two ways. The Roman God had two faces, one looking into the past and the other into the future. This symbolized both hope for the future yet also tinged with some fear and apprehension, and thanksgiving for that which had gone before. This could also be a dual thing of both gratitude and warm memories for the good past experiences, together with a sense of relief and gratitude that the bad experiences were over, and had been survived. From this illustration of the two-way look it is easy to imagine how confusing, complex, and, at times, contradictory being in this stage of faith can be.

The contradictions lie in the fact of this stage being one in which a formation is taking place. The process of this formation is one in which experiences and attitudes of the past are sifted and analyzed, not always objectively, but also at times experientially, by actually living them out in the present. Together with this looking backwards, there is also a looking forwards to the possibilities of what could be and would endure. This is expressed in idealism that is fuelled by a conviction that despite bad things in the past that previous generations inflicted upon them, people will make sure things are better when they enter the future and determine its outcomes. This attitude is often lived out by those at this stage, acting out in the present their hopes for a future that has not yet arrived.

For this stage to be worked through successfully, an adequate formation or 'Faith Package' that will enable the individual to enter into their future has to be put together. This 'Faith Package' is in essence a set of principles, ideals and guidelines against which all future faith experiences will be evaluated before being incorporated into, or ejected from, any future formulation of faith. This is more or less carried with us for the rest of our life and used often, especially during times of change and crisis. In the confusion that the process of doing this causes, we need stable factors, or fixed points of reference outside the individual, but available to them. These points of reference are twofold: *The peer group* and *the mature adult world.*

b) *The peer group*

This is the group of those at the same stage in faith development that is the milieu in which the working out is done. This group is also very powerful as a testing ground for the faith package or set of beliefs. Nothing that does not conform to the generally accepted criteria of the group has much chance of being incorporated into the belief system that will carry the individual on into the future. A very important value of those at this stage of development is group loyalty. This is understandable from a point of view of security. To be in the process of working something out that will carry one into an unknown future is very frightening. Although it is tempting to look back to experiences of earlier stages that were good, these cannot necessarily of themselves be viable in the future, nor on the other hand can they be easily cast aside. Therefore group solidarity rules so that individual security might be achieved.

Again I illustrate the power of this group loyalty, or solidarity, from my own experience as a youth club leader. In one group I led there was an outbreak of disappearing light bulbs, especially in the toilets. When it became particularly bad I became angry and said to the whole assembled group, 'Come on, who did it? This has gone too far.' The response was a stony silence and the more I pressed, the stronger I felt the resistance in the silence. They were expressing loyalty in the face of adult threat by strong group solidarity. When I perceived this I changed my tack. 'Alright,' I said, 'Forget it, but I do expect you to be sensible and see that all those bulbs are back and working, because if they are not it will lead to problems that might rebound on you.' I then deliberately took a low profile for a while, and within a very short time the bulbs were all working and the same problem did not happen again.

This illustration of how a peer group works demonstrates two things. The first is that within itself it can achieve a great deal. Just as the simple problem of replacing light bulbs was achieved by the group internally, so also can belief systems or faith packages that are sound and workable for individuals be worked out. I have experienced people, now adults, who were in groups I led when they were adolescent, making statements about faith that they now hold dearly and have worked out for themselves. I recognize in these statements a sound and deep understanding, which I don't remember communicating to them during their adolescence, but which they claim began during those times through my influence.

The second point is the importance of the sincerely available more mature person against whom the adolescent, as an individual or in a group, can interact and pit wits. This is what the group was doing in the case of the light bulbs. I was responding as a mature available adult in a way that enabled them to problem-solve.

c) *The mature available person*

At this point I do not wish to say much about this mature facilitator of development, because I think it more appropriate to deal with it in conclusions to this faith development stage. It is, however, a very important issue in faith development at all stages, but especially so at this one, though perhaps less so in the later ones. The fact is that as human beings we all need such points of reference in an enabling way for faith to develop. We can only live fully as individuals in relationship with others, and the importance of the mature enabling person as a significant other is especially evident when we examine this stage of development.

8.3 The 'synthetic' task

This is the word that describes the main task of those at this stage of faith. Our focus so far has been with the conditions required for the task to be accomplished. When that happens, the person is in a position to move on. But as we shall see later, not everyone does move on, because this stage of faith seems to be one at which it is convenient, or perhaps comfortable, for people to stay in for life, and many do so.

The task, described by the word 'synthetic', is that of putting together a 'Faith Package' that suits the individual. Such a 'package' is made up of two kinds of material. The major part is from the past, consisting of faith values from each of the previous stages that still make sense and work in a practical way for the individual. The second, albeit minor part, consists of new ideas, experiences and information that come from the adult world, which are often used to test the validity of that which comes from previous stages. However, the testing is usually not very thorough, but it must be adequate enough to allow the individual to have an operational faith for the present time. A more thorough testing and sifting of material from the childhood stages of faith comes at a later stage of development when material rejected at this stage is taken up again and reintegrated.

Again, a crucial factor at this stage of development is the quality of what has gone before. Those with less than adequate childhood faith nurture will have more difficulties in working out a satisfactory form of faith for they lack the foundations from which to do so. This results in an inability to cope realistically with all the new ideas being thrust at them by the wider world into which they are now entering. The result is that, through their insecurity, they take in more of the new ideas than is healthy, and are a prey to extremists and exploiters of all kinds. Unbalanced religious sects, the drug scene and extremist political groups tend to sweep up such people.

By inadequate faith nurture in childhood I do not only mean those with none at all, but also those who have had an oppressive faith nurture that is not sensitive to the nature of children and makes demands of them that are too great. St. Augustine's words (in *City of God*, Book XII, chapter 13) ring true concerning this:

> If a child's upbringing is adjusted to its strength, it will grow and become capable of further progress; but if it is strained beyond its capacity it will fade away before it has a chance to grow up.

Furthermore, of insensitive pharisaical practices Jesus said:

> "It is better for a millstone to be tied round their neck and they

> be thrown into the sea lest they offend one of these little ones who believe in me." This emphasizes the vulnerability of children in their early lives. Hence the forms of nurture they receive have powerful effects on faith development. The negatives as well as the positives play a very dominant role in the synthetic process at this stage of faith. It is then quite reasonable that Jesus, a man of faith, should speak so strongly against those who harm faith at its most vulnerable stage of growth. (Bible references: Matthew 18:6, 7; and Luke 17:1, 2.)

In conclusion, it is at the synthetic stage of faith development that people are at their most vulnerable as well as at their most creative. Those who have had good childhood faith nurture, together with wise teachers and role models who are available to them throughout the whole period of the stage, will be able to put together a sound and balanced *personal, not second-hand,* faith package to carry them into the future. Those who lack these things will be handicapped. They will tend in the extreme to be either rebellious and negative, or passive and withdrawn; either joining unsound and unhealthy sects or political movements, or just become aimless drifters who believe in nothing because they can trust nobody.

8.4 The 'conventional' aspect

The word 'conventional' describes the process by which the faith package is put together. A convention is a group of people who have been convened, that is called together by an authority outside of themselves. This convention is given the power to make decisions, draw up statements of common belief, and devise laws or rules, all of which are validated by common consent of the convened group.

How does this apply to those at this stage of faith development? It would seem to me that the main authority would be the need that arises from the stage of human development in which these people now are. They are no longer children who depend upon authority figures, such as parents, for their security. They therefore have to discover an authoritative support system for themselves. Their inner energies propelling them on to become adults in their own right demands that the way in which this is done must be by means of peer group activity. However, this cannot take place without some reference to, and respect for, the faith statements of adult authorities. Those mature authorities, who have themselves successfully moved beyond this stage of faith development, are sensed as being available in a meaningful way to the 'conventional' peer group.

The process that takes place in this peer group convention is one of trial and error, experiment and discussion, taking both the material from earlier stages and the input from external authorities. This is sifted, tested and valued. That which does not appeal or have immediate value is rejected, and that which is accepted by the peer group convention is eventually put together in a coherent form as a suitable faith package. This is then seen as the norm for the group and becomes very strongly binding on them all. Conformity to this faith package signifies the end of this stage, and people will stay in this very conforming mode as long as the faith package is workable for them, or until they have a strong enough sense of their own individual identity together with a robust well-being, which will enable them to question it.

When these things happen the person is then at the beginning of the next (fifth) faith development stage, known as the 'individuative-reflective' stage. Sadly, because of lack of well-being and varieties of anxiety, many never seem to have the initiative to move on. Hence stage four can too easily become a comfortable resting place for life. Later we look at the many problems that arise out of that reality.

8.5 A summary of the nature and varieties of synthetic-conventional faith

This section is by way of being a summary in which all that has been said about Synthetic Conventional Faith will be drawn together as a whole. There are three main points that give a focus to an understanding of this stage of faith, but the fundamental issue that is being worked out is that of acquiring a 'Faith Package' that will serve for the rest of one's life. Although this is never fully achieved, as the later stages will show clearly. Many people acquire a large number of aspects of faith at this stage that do last for the remainder of their lives, becoming more adequately integrated as they pass through subsequent stages. The sad thing is that there are also considerable numbers of people who just stick here at stage four and think that they have 'arrived'. We will now look at the three points that define the nature of this stage. They will be put in question form because finding answers to questions concerning the big issues of life is the main definitive statement for this stage.

i) *In whom or what can we put our trust?*

Everyone becomes aware at some stage of their life, as they grow into adulthood, that they are not totally self-sufficient. Not only is a point of reference outside ourselves needed to give us an identity and bring security, but also we never cease to need someone to do things for us that we cannot do for ourselves. When we get beyond the need for parenting, certain aspects of parental need remain. Hence the existence of all kinds of helping professions, pastoral, medical, legal, religious, therapeutic, or even just a good friend. Can we trust these people? Or do we need something beyond them such as 'a god'? Perhaps we make a god of some of these other people, or even a theory about life, a philosophy based upon science, history, politics, 'watch your own back', and so on. The fact is that we all need something to believe in that has a degree of objectivity of some kind. At the synthetic conventional stage we either discover such an object of faith, or create one, and the basis of it lies within its trustworthiness as perceived at the time. I say this because should it fail to be trustworthy at a later stage, it will be rejected and some other object of faith sought around which a new 'Faith Package' will be constructed.

ii) *How can we support each other in sustaining this faith?*
This expresses the strong conventional aspect of this stage. There is a great need to join with others in putting together the 'Faith Package' because to do it alone is impossible; the level of vulnerability being so high that individuals need to belong to and act through groups. Being a card-carrying member of a group, movement, or organization is the main feature expressing this need for support through group activity. This is evident among student groups and also the way that religious and political movements all have their clubs and societies. Through their debates, rituals, meetings and social gatherings, support is given to those who have committed themselves to the faith or 'ideology' held within the group, while at the same time the more uncertain and less committed have an arena in which to work out their own faith. As people grow older this need becomes less, as whatever 'Faith Package' is acquired at this stage becomes more soundly developed. Another aspect of the support and sustenance required at this stage is the place of the 'guru'. Adults of mature age and confidence in their own 'Faith Package', which is acceptable to these conventional groups, become revered guides, heroes, authors of the right books to read, or speakers on the circuit of meetings, conferences and assemblies.

iii) *How can we defend the faith so essential for our well-being?*
A very large amount of energy is always invested in the defense of the faith held by people at the synthetic conventional stage. This is because the personal 'Faith Packages' at this stage of

development are always new, fragile, and yet untested by experience. The process of defense also serves to hone, refine and develop the package, so that this energy invested in defense is also an investment in development. As people grow older they normally feel less and less need to be defensive, especially if they have worked out a sound and workable faith. It might be that the 'Faith Package' acquired at this stage was totally rejected and, later on, a more suitable one put together, or that the synthetic-conventional one had within it the potential to be developed and modified without the need for rejection.

Whatever the case, to remain in a state of faith insecurity, needing to put much energy into defense, is always a sign of faith immaturity in adults, and an indication concerning why quite large numbers of people stick at this fourth stage of faith. By using these three questions I suggest that we have a good general diagnostic tool for recognizing those at this stage of faith.

In order to enable recognition of some finer points we next need some examples.

8.6 Varieties of synthetic-conventional faith

The main purpose for giving the following examples is to demonstrate three very important aspects of the nature of synthetic-conventional faith which will help in understanding more fully its place in people's lives, and hopefully, recognizing it in ourselves as well as in others.

The first is the wide variety that there is at this level of faith, and believe that it exists in everyone to a greater or lesser degree. Even those who claim to have no faith at all will find that they do so, in something or other, but have yet to recognize it as being faith.

The second is that we all make projections onto people, objects, or even fantasy people, objects or ideas, and, as we have noted, that this is an essential part of our nature and need as human beings. The important issue at this level of faith is the basis in trust or non-trust from which the projections are being made; and these have a definite relationship to our earlier nurture.

The third factor is to discern within the synthetic-convention faith package elements of enduring reliability that last beyond this stage and become parts of later stages. It is these elements that give security to the person, and by so doing enable them to move on creatively in faith. Where these do not exist, or are very weak at this stage, then the future, faithwise, is traumatic. It often leads to this stage being converted into a very narrow and dogmatic fundamentalism that is vigorously and, in some cases, violently guarded. It also has a strong element of paranoia because the fear element in the individual is high, and is usually based upon a fear of non-existence as a person. So we now look at a few examples of the various types of synthetic-conventional faith.

i) *Faith based upon a scientific mythology*

Just about the most common current example of this is 'Darwinism' or the 'Theory of Evolution'. Although Darwin's ideas and scientific discoveries are the basis of the mythology of this faith, its main initiator was Thomas Huxley. When we examine the contents of this particular faith package, it can be seen as being fairly standard synthetic-conventional for several reasons. Firstly, it has an accepted mythology held by its followers that does have a degree of support in objective facts. Such as the fact that there is a missing link, namely, that if mankind did evolve from apes it can only be a projection at the moment based upon certain elements of evidence available which seem to point that way, because there is no concrete evidence that puts the issue beyond doubt. Secondly, the faith package built upon the mythology has the power to motivate people emotionally in such a way that they are willing to spend enormous amounts of energy looking for the missing link. This leads to the third point, which is that the vigor and fervor with which the mythology is defended against contrary evidence, and the obvious rejoicing that takes place when even fragments of supporting evidence are found, would indicate that it is more of a religion, which its adherents need to believe in, than a coldly rational scientific theory. To illustrate this point I refer to some correspondence on this subject in *The Tablet,* from March through May 1996.

In the March edition a Dr. Le Fanu wrote an article about a newly discovered small creature that lives on the lips of a lobster. In this article he argued that certain facts about this creature were contrary to those biological facts that were used to support the 'Darwinian Faith'. I read the article but did not find it very interesting, or even feel that it was very important. I am very neutral as far as such things are concerned, and really don't care much either way. However, in the April edition there appeared a letter from a current media celebrity, Prof. Richard Dawkins, which was a very strident and emotional attack on the contents of Dr. Le Fanu's article on the grounds that it dared to question the basic foundations of Darwinism. I saw this response as being that of a person whose synthetic-conventional faith was under attack, and not as a reasoned scientific response. These are the reasons why I think this is so.

a) Statements in Dawkins' letter were emotional and 'nit-picking'. He takes several sentences to say that the name of this creature was not properly written in Le Fanu's article. It should be *Symbion pandora* and not *Symbion Pandora*. He also takes Le Fanu to task for saying that someone whom he called Miles Eldredge was in fact Niles Eldredge and from this writes the whole article off on the ground that someone who makes such mistakes cannot be capable of understanding biology.

b) In the second half of the letter Dawkins claims that the discovery of this creature does not challenge Darwinism at all. Although most evolutionary history is hidden from us, he says, there is other evidence that is overwhelmingly strong in its favor.

I see this as simply a statement of faith, and not a scientific response to a new discovery.

c) The concluding sentence of the letter is very standard synthetic-conventional evangelism. After attempting to show how ignorant and ill informed Dr. Le Fanu's article was, and in the process quoting titles of his own works, Dawkins says, 'I hesitate to recommend my own stuff, but Dr. Le Fanu appears to need all the enlightenment he can get.'

My impression of all this is that Prof. Dawkins is doing what we all do when at the synthetic-conventional stage of faith, namely defend it with vigor whenever it is challenged. We do this because that is the nature of things, and when it no longer works for us we move on to the next stage of faith. Vigorous defense is a sign of uncertainty, and that perhaps the need to move on is just beginning to show itself. The real issues are often covered up in this kind of debate, but are all to do with needing faith, and why we need to express this need in a particular way. *The use of science in the package has to do with the psychology of the individual in the area of trust.* This applies to all faith objects. In this case, Dawkins' faith is based upon the trustworthiness of the scientific method, and this was being threatened by Le Fanu.

ii) *Faith based in folk religion*

This is probably the most widely spread kind of synthetic-conventional faith packages. It would include ancient pagan religions, Animism and popular forms of Hinduism. In rural England it is often the basis of actual practical faith in people who would describe themselves as 'Church of England'. The basic set of beliefs goes something like this:

> I know that there is a power out there greater than myself; though I recognize it, and know I have a high degree of dependence upon it being favorable towards me, I cannot fully understand or define it.

Out of this basic belief come a wide variety of religious practices that are used to make the individual feel that they are giving respect to this power, and thereby keeping in favor with it. I find this interesting because I see in it a very basic, and often honest, awareness of being human in relation to one's environment. I am myself very aware, in moments of reflection and being in touch with my basic humanity, that there still exists in me some of this, even though I have moved beyond it now, and on its own find it unsatisfying; I think that elements of it will remain with me all my life.

The reasons why I have moved beyond such a faith package are all expressed in St. Augustine's '*City of God*' book VII. In this the author discusses the Roman Paganism of his day, to show that it is based upon a projection of human need onto objects in the natural world. The needs are real, but the objects onto which they are projected have no power of themselves in a deeper spiritual sense. Therefore they trap the individual into an ultimately inadequate faith, and thereby inhibit their personal growth. St. Paul says the same thing in the first chapter of his letter to the Romans in a graphically more powerful way, in accordance with his own personality:

> They exchanged the glory of the immortal God for a worthless imitation, for the image of mortal man, of birds, quadrupeds and reptiles.

Paul's argument goes on to show the moral decline which can come out of this folk religion or paganism. This can be observed in history the whole world over. A modern example of this is how Himmler sought to revive pre-Christian paganism as a spiritual basis for Nazism. He claimed that it was the Jewish and Christian tradition that so weakened the Nazi idea of Germans as a super-race. Hence both must be eliminated and replaced by a vigorous and violent form of paganism. This would motivate

Germany so that its forces, led by the SS, would conquer the world. One must give Himmler credit for seeing that a spiritually based faith could be a powerful motivator, but what an evil one he chose, and what a disastrous end it had.

But now let us now return to our main purpose, citing examples of the stage of synthetic-conventional faith, having a real validity in faith development, but which may become disastrous for many who become rigidly stuck within them.

As an example of modern, very basic folk faith without any sophistication, the following report of a conversation with an elderly countryman is interesting. He told me that he did not believe in the Church, or any clever stuff educated people said, for he totally believed in the sun as the source of all power, for without it nothing would grow or exist, including himself. All his life he believed this. He did his garden and kept out of religion, politics and all other fanciful things. This made him feel happy and secure. The sun was real because he could see it, and he also could see how it affected everything. This was his faith. My feeling was, but I did not say so, that he could continue to hold this faith as long as he lived where he did, in the protective environment of a country estate with a wealthy and understanding master in the form of the local squire. Perhaps radical social change would be the only thing that would precipitate him out of this narrow and very dogmatic faith. In essence his faith package was only operational for the time being, within the context of his present social conditions, thereby showing the limitations of many synthetic-conventional faith situations.

I have also come across variations on this theme in people like sailors and miners; people whose work brings home to them their vulnerability and need for a greater power to protect them. When I was a curate in the Forest of Dean I had many conversations with miners, especially ones pensioned off with diseases like pneumosilicosis. They all spoke of praying when underground, and giving thanks for their safety. Very few had anything to do with formal organized religion, but they all had this basic type of faith. Farmers live less dangerous lives, but they also have this awareness of some greater power on whom they, like it or not, are dependent for their livelihood. I find it an interesting fact that prayers are often said at National Farmers Union meetings.

At this point it is appropriate to say that the kind of folk religion I have been describing does not have rigid boundaries set by being or not being a member of an institution like the Church of England. I have come across many people who are definitely 'C of E', but whose synthetic-conventional faith package is virtually the same as the sun worshipper. Some could be churchwardens who are also farmers; others quite sophisticated people in many ways, socially and intellectually, but in matters of faith have a 'God' who is particularly their own, who say such things as, 'My God is…', and see others as having an equally valid God who may not be like theirs, but one upon whom they call when in need. Such people would say things like, 'Let everyone call on his own God in his own way and we will all be happy.' I see these people as having much in common with the Roman pagans described by Augustine in *City of God* and very little in common with the dominant theologies of the Church of England.

My final example of this folk religion within the context of an institution would be that of many people's belief about infant baptism. It is quite simple. Many people want their infants baptized because they say, 'They will do better.' That is the totality of the belief system behind it. They hold to this firmly and cannot be moved. When questioned, the usual response is an emotional one indicating its synthetic-conventional nature. Such people can never enter into any form of discussion about the theology of baptism in any way. They just say: we know it works, we want it for our child and you as the parson must do it for us.

iii) *Faith based on an intellectual structure*
This form of synthetic-conventional faith package is one to be found among intellectuals and academics. Because its contents are very well worked out, and can be supported easily by argument with others of the same ability and background, they are usually sustainable for life if one allows for a reasonable amount of modification, as the holder grows older. They do, however, have the weakness in that they are very 'ivory tower' and they 'ghetto-ize' the holder within a certain social group. The power of the 'ghetto-izing' process can be so great that there comes a point in their lives when those in this faith situation lose all meaningful contact with those outside their own social group. There is always the tendency for such people to become very rigidly sectarian.

General examples of this kind of synthetic-conventional faith are to be seen in denominationalism within the Christian Church. All denominations try to put Jesus Christ within a specific frame, and then build a theology around this frame. Each frame contains something in common with all other frames, but at the same time excludes or includes something that makes the composition of the picture slightly different in each case. The contents of the picture is then sustained and defended by argument, and each individual picture is seen by those faithful to it as being the whole truth. This is very synthetic-conventional, and, as in the case of scientific mythological faith, the basis motivating the arguments in defense of these positions is emotional, and based upon need.

I would cite as examples of this the various groupings within the Church of England such as Anglo Catholics, Evangelicals and Broad Church. Calvinism is another. Movements like the Latin Mass group within the Roman Catholic Church and the Prayer Book Society within the Church of England are others. What interests me is the fact that some people get into these groupings and stay for life, being totally loyal to their specific group, supporting and defending it and relating to people in other groups with varying degrees of attitudes, from a 'live and let live' respect, to downright hostility. Some will move from one to another 'clique' and find satisfaction, whereas others move out of them, or become very loosely attached as they grow older.

These realities all have to do with an individual's emotional and spiritual growth, about how safe they feel to be themselves and move outside frameworks that are in some ways similar to a playpen! It is within the context of a supportive framework that we are free to experiment and discover ourselves and the basis of our faith. We need this very much, but if we really grow in confidence and faith while in the playpen, there must come a time when we climb out of it. This does not render the playpen invalid; it is indicative of its relevance. A good playpen experience gives us the ability to live with confidence outside it; a bad one does not. A good experience makes us value it for what it has given us, a bad one can make us hate or fear it.

I meet many people who tell me of their experiences, faithwise, of these groupings. I find that they fall generally into three groups. In the first group are those who once belonged to one of them, but has now moved out, having a dynamic faith, yet still respecting the group they left for what they received, but moved out because they wanted more than it could supply. The second kind of person moved out and now hates the group they once belonged to, as having a very negative, inadequate faith in that it does not really work for them and has left them in a very painful emotional state. In the third instance are those who stay within one of these groups and cannot see any reason for moving outside at all. They also tend to have a great deal of fear and find the group supportive. These are obviously generalizations, but they say something important about this kind of synthetic-conventional faith-stage. Such groups are very important, even essential, for people's faith development, but they need to be of a good quality and led by competent people who have an honest awareness of their wider place in the development of faith.

iv) *Faith based upon a 'charismatic' personality*
A very obvious example of this is the Jesus Movement that was very popular among the young of the USA. in the 1960s. It was a group movement in rebellion against the established churches that saw them as corrupt and worldly, and sought to form a more spiritually pure group that just focused on the person of Jesus Christ. At the same time in England the young were going to India to find 'gurus', as a way of doing the same sort of thing. In the secular world, Marxists idealize Karl Marx and Trotskyites Trotsky.

In most cases the building of a synthetic-conventional faith around an idealized person is a reaction against institutions perceived to be corrupt. For example, as the Soviet System began to decline because of corruption and inbuilt weaknesses, the purist Marxist would defend his faith by saying that the system had moved away from its founder, Marx, and therefore a return to the pure teaching of Marx would correct things. In the Christian Church we see an example of this in a book by J. Middleton Murry, written in the period between the two world wars called, *The Betrayal of Christ by the Churches*. In it Murry takes a very pacifist stand seeing this as the position Jesus Christ would take, and which the institutional churches were betraying.

There are, however, examples of those who hold onto a synthetic-conventional faith, while at the same time continuing to live within a more complex faith system. I have in mind one Gabrielle Bossis, whose book *He and I* is a diary of her very personal spiritual relationship with Jesus Christ. This is obviously the essence of her faith and yet it is held within the context of the Roman Catholic Church's institutions and not in opposition to them. I cite this as a case of a synthetic-conventional faith system with a content that has the potential, and actual ability, to move on outside it. Therefore, Gabrielle Bossis should not be understood as having just a synthetic-conventional faith package, but as having had such a package which she could move beyond without having to abandon it. I see this as one of the marks of genuine catholicism in its widest sense – that it has the ability to develop and absorb new spiritual experiences within its basic faith system, without losing or abandoning its original essentials.

v) *Faith in an institution*

I see this in general as the antithesis of the previous synthetic-conventional faith package. It tends to be held by a certain type of person who cannot cope with much intimacy of personal relationships. The first example of this that comes to mind is a retired bank manager I once knew. He used to speak with great reverence of 'The Bank' as though this institution was God himself. He had spent his whole life in it and it had provided him with everything. Therefore he had always been its loyal and obedient servant. He also viewed the Church to which he belonged in the same way. What deeply mattered to him were such things as: how people dressed, the way the liturgy was conducted, and the status of people within its hierarchy. He was very rigid, and only felt safe when things were done properly and the right 'conventional' procedures carried out.

For such people, any faults, failures or changes within the institution they have deified are traumatic and life threatening. In churches such people oppose new liturgies, new translations of the Bible and other changes of an institutional nature, vigorously opposing them, and forming societies to preserve the status quo. Examples of this, previously mentioned, are the Prayer Book Society in the Church of England and the Latin Mass movement within the Roman Catholic Church.

The main problem I see with this kind of synthetic-conventional faith package is its basic intransigence and lack of tolerance. Seemingly it is not possible for those in this category to move on without abandoning their basic credo. Hence they are stuck people in terms of their potential for spiritual growth. Unable to consider anything new to take forward with them, so vital in enabling faith to grow, such people are vulnerable and easily threatened. They use up excessive amounts of energy to maintain their faith position, a very debilitating long-term prospect, illustrating that a healthy synthetic-conventional 'Faith Package' must always be one which contains elements that can be taken on into later stages of development.

vi) *Faith in a political system*

This can more easily be seen in extreme political ideologies such as Fascism and Marxism. More moderate and workable political systems are always largely pragmatic but based on certain principles. Two such examples of this are 'One Nation Conservatism' and 'Social Democracy'. Politicians who hold such political views tend to have a faith outside their political system and see the political party in which they work as being a vehicle for carrying out in practice their other and often more deeply held beliefs. One example of this is the Christian Socialist Movement.

Such politicians would, at times when the political party to which they belong moves away from their deeper beliefs, either leave it or modify the political system to accommodate their principles. One good example of this was Sir Robert Peel's actions in repealing the Corn Laws, even though this went against the beliefs and interests of his Party. He did it because to do so was in the interests of the poor of the country and in line with the Christian principle of charity. In modern times Emma Nicholson left the Conservative Party for similar reasons of principle. In both cases I would claim that their faith package was rooted in something outside, and greater than, their political party group. Emma Nicholson was reacting against the narrow, destructive and very immature political belief package generally known as 'Thatcherism', which was in respects similar to a fascist-type synthetic-conventional faith system, imposing its dogmas onto the world in which it lives, seemingly without a wider awareness of that world and all its complexities.

This kind of factor of an imposed faith, even against all the facts and conditions in the world in which it is set, is something of an indicator that such a political system of beliefs is, in its essential nature, conventional-synthetic. It is also conventional-synthetic of the worst kind because it cannot grow and develop in response to its environment. Its believing followers are trapped in a very destructive situation in which strong elements of denial are essential if they are to maintain it. Because of this, more and more energy goes into propaganda and all other means of denial aimed at boosting the faith of the believers against the odds. After creating much pain and havoc, such faith systems eventually collapse, because they do not have within them the energy to be creative over a long period of time. In history we see many examples of this, such as the Fascists of Germany and Italy, Franco's Spain, Communist Russia, and Chairman Mao's 'cultural revolution' in China.

There are two very important observations to be made from these examples of politically based faith packages that apply to all types of synthetic-convention stages of faith. They are, firstly, that the simpler and more obviously immediate answer that they offer to the potential believer, then the greater the appeal to those at this stage of development. Therefore they will always have an appeal, especially to those who are insecure and not adequately nurtured at previous stages. The second is that because they do not have any transcendent content, that is, they are closed and dogmatic systems, they do not contain any elasticity that could enable growth and development into a faith that is able to cope with changing conditions. This last point is a good indicator of the quality of a faith suitable for those at this stage, because it must contain within it elements that are essential for it to move on. If this is not so the synthetic-conventional faith package ceases to be one of faith in its fullest sense. At worst, it be becomes a destructive trap.

8.7 Concluding remarks on Stage 4 – an invitation

Now the reader is invited to reflect upon his or her own faith. So doing will make one's understanding more realistic by rooting it in personal experience.

A very important skill required for faith development is the ability of self-reflection upon one's own experiences. Also generally needed is someone further along the road of faith than ourselves to act as a spiritual mirror, reflecting back to us what they see in our present understanding of where we are faithwise. Such a person must have the maturity and ability to listen and feed back what they hear without being parental, dogmatic and prescriptive. The following exercise is given for this stage of development, because this is the first stage of adult faith, and as such a crucial one. Prior to this fourth stage such a reflective exercise would not be relevant, or even possible. But at this stage, and beyond, it becomes essential.

Following are four italicized questions that guide the personal reflection:

a) *What was my personal faith package at this stage of my life?*
To answer this question look back to the time of your adolescence. Note down what was believed then, and form it into a faith package. You may find that there was more than one faith package at that time.

In my own experience I had two basic 'packages'. The first one, as a student was political. I was in a state of atheism and rebellion and believed that Marxism would put the world right. This left me very empty quite quickly, and also I noted that hard core Marxists I met were not very nice people. After a year or so

I had an evangelical conversion experience. I became a Christian by choice and built up a fairly standard evangelical faith package. The basics of this have stayed with my all my life, but it has developed and changed by taking into it other spheres of enrichment. Now, in my mid-seventies, I have become more mystical and contemplative with a widely based 'catholic' outlook, but am still aware of some elements of the original faith package.

I would say that two important factors in my synthetic conventional experience were, firstly the influence of the authority figures who were experienced within the two faith systems. The Marxist ones were very negative, but the Christian ones were positive. Secondly, the nature of the Christian, evangelical-type faith package I put together was such that it allowed for development and modification. It gave me a basic platform of faith from which, as I grew and experienced new things, they could be positively absorbed into it, modifying and changing it without having to abandon the basics. In short, as I matured I became more catholic (but not a Roman Catholic) in the fullest meaning of the word.

b) *Have I grown beyond my conventional-synthetic faith, or even ditched it?*

Many people do not grow beyond this stage. The likelihood is that if you have not grown beyond it you are in need of help in developing your self-reflective skills, and this exercise will be painful for you. You may indeed feel very angry at being asked this question, not least if you feel you have ditched what was your whole package.

c) *Does my present faith contain any of my synthetic-conventional faith package?*

Some adults have to totally reject their synthetic/conventional faith package because it did not contain enough flexibility. If you are one of these, then you no doubt will have gone through, or are still in, a painful period of loss of faith, beset by much uncertainty.

d) *Who or what were my authorities to whom I referred for support in my synthetic-conventional faith, and who are they now?*
This is asked because we all need referencing 'authorities' in whatever stage of faith we are. Though these can be very varied and change as we grow older, it is, however, good to know of them. For my part I recognize a move over the years from people such as parental figures, leaders of groups, authorities in certain subjects, whom I deemed to be 'experts', and famous figures from history whom I admired, to God as revealed through Jesus Christ in the four Gospels. I would say that now my faith centers on reading the four Gospels, praying and meditating upon them and asking the Holy Spirit to help me perceive the world in which I live through the eyes of Jesus whom I believe to be the only truly good and reliable person that ever lived. Others have their value, but feel to me rather less reliable. Many others are inadequate and most are almost totally unreliable. It is possible in this last statement to see strong elements of synthetic-conventional faith, but as will be seen when we look at further stages of faith development, the person of Jesus Christ has a broader dimension than is popularly portrayed. He is much more than the many statements people make about Him indicate. The burning issue for me at this phase of my life journey is to know Him as he really is and not as I have been told he is (see Psalm 17:16; and 1 Corinthians 13:9-12).

I realize that I have just expressed very strong emotions about other people, and that this arises from my own neurotic self. This deep mistrust is still there within me, but there is a more positive side. It is that it is normal for the young to idealize adults as part of their development, and it is also normal to experience some degree of disillusionment when one becomes old enough to realize that one's childhood and adolescent heroes have feet of clay. However, for spiritual health it is essential to move beyond all this, seeing people as they really are, and accept them as they really are. This is love with maturity. It is all about loving and being loved with no strings attached. The basis of the Christian Gospel is one of relationships based on love and forgiveness that brings about redemption. This is only possible when faith goes beyond trust and high expectations of other human beings, to trust in a higher power that transcends the human scene; in short, a practical and living trust in God. Only then are we freed from our past hurts and present inadequacies to be able to love fully and not, as most of us do, in a limited and very conditional way.

I have had to spend all my life praying for grace to love, and the more this grace is given, the more I love in the fullest sense of the word. This gives an enabling power to accept other human beings as they are, warts and all. I am sure that it is a growth into the next stages of faith development that enables this to happen. Remember, Jesus said, 'Unless your righteousness shall exceed that of the scribes and Pharisees, you cannot enter the kingdom of heaven.' [St. Matthew's Gospel 5:7.] Pharisaic faith was in general very synthetic-conventional, so let us therefore move on!

Chapter 9

Stage 5 – The Individuative-Reflective Adult Phase

This fifth stage of faith development begins when one's experiences of life begin to conflict with one's synthetic-conventional 'faith package'. Questions are raised when what we experience cannot be squared with what we actually believe as the received truth in our existing faith package. This sets off within us thought processes, which often start by trying to rationalize the uncomfortable experiences in such a way that they can be fitted into our received faith system. This can work to a point, and help us to hold onto the received package, but, whereas the individual holding the faith does not readily see the absurdity of what they believe, a non-involved observer can. At this early point in the development of this stage a person becomes extremely vigorous in defense of the previous one, often obsessively so. The less there is of durable content in the existing synthetic-conventional faith package, the greater the tendency towards obsessive and even absurd defense there is. The reason for this is that in such cases much more of past faith belief and practice has to be abandoned, and this causes greater grief and pain.

For a person to enter this next stage fully the time has to come when defense of the previous stage stops and rejection of it takes place. The rejection has to be quite definite and wholesale to start with, but later on bits of the previous stage are taken back and integrated into the new stage. What people are doing at this stage of faith development is simply making a faith their own as opposed to accepting uncritically the faith imposed upon them by their inheritance and culture. Having stated in outline the general nature of this stage of faith, let us now fill in a few details and flesh it out.

Firstly, it is important to observe that the intellect plays the main role now. Everything in the received 'synthetic-conventional' faith package is questioned by the means of rationality. 'Does it work and make sense for me now?' is the big question. When people ask this they are giving a very clear signal that they are moving from the synthetic-conventional stage of faith into this new one. To help such people one must encourage the questioning by making them feel safe to do so, and at the same time encouraging them to work out the consequences of the questioning. Being defensive of whatever is being questioned or rejected at this stage is destructive, leading either to a false guilt or to a violent rejection of everything, in which 'the baby is thrown out with the bath water'. It destroys faith rather than helps it to grow.

The needs of people at this stage of faith are twofold. Firstly it is to have all that they share accepted in a non-judgmental way. The right response is to reflect back what is said, followed by a question that will stimulate further thought. So often the implications of what is said are not fully realized, and until it is forward movement and growth cannot take place. It is possible to stick at this stage and spend one's life going round and round in circles. Sound spiritual direction is essential at such times, and so this is the second requirement. However, guidance must be sensitive. This means the person aiding direction, not 'giving directions', must be at least a stage further on, so that they have worked out satisfactorily all possible issues likely to be raised for themselves. That enables good guides not to be threatened by anything that might come out in the dialogue and so forced into a negative, defensive stance.

Those going into this stage are always argumentative and predominantly interested in the intellectual aspect related to faith. Because of this anyone not mature enough in listening will be trapped into futile intellectual arguments of a debating nature. The issue then becomes who won and who lost the argument. This kind of situation is so simplistic, immature and unproductive that it does not meet the real need of those at this stage of faith to work matters out for themselves. We all need a faith that satisfies us, and works for us in a day-to-day practical way. What therefore is needed is the right stimulus to move into this, not simple idealistic ideas that do not satisfy when tested out in everyday life. The objective is not to produce a set of ideals into which one twists and amends the everyday experience of living so that the facts of life are continually being distorted to fit them, but an *inward dynamic* faith that gives the grace to live a satisfying lifestyle that relates honestly to them. The only creative way, therefore, is to put to such people the right kind of searching question, and then leave them to wrestle with it. This tends to be a very slow and often frustrating process, but that is the nature of the struggle and it has to be accepted.

So far we have seen that the intellect appears dominant at this stage. Whereas no doubt this is true, the fact is that there is more to it than this. Intellectual argument and satisfaction are of prime importance, but this is more a means than an end. That is why I have pointed out the trap of thinking that people at this stage just need to sort out the intellectual aspect of faith and nothing else. To do this is to be very superficial because beneath all the intellectual activity something very emotional is going on, and the intellect is struggling hard to express this in words that fit and make sense. It is crucial to recognize this, what I will call 'the emotional undertow'.

9.1 The emotional undertow

The emotional undertow to the intellectual struggle characteristic of the stage 4 to 5 transition during adulthood can be summed up in one word first coined by properly famed psychiatrist, Carl Jung, that of '*individuation*'. The process of individuation is one that describes personal psychological growth in the second half of life. It happens over a period of time and begins at the individuative-reflective stage of faith, but is completed during the next one. At this stage the intellectual tools are sharpened up and the ground prepared so that the deep work can be carried out during the next stage. For deep and meaningful inner psychological and spiritual work to take place a good intellectual framework of understanding is necessary. The intellect needs to be equipped so that it is used as a tool for enabling growth of the whole person and not as a means of creating and using defense mechanisms against the pain of growth.

The *Baker Encyclopedia of Psychology* gives the following definition of the process of individuation:

> A Jungian concept denoting the process by which a person becomes a psychological individual, an indivisible unity or whole. This process of self-realization involves differentiating a totality called the self from all the components of the personality. Thus, individuation is a synthetic process of integrating all the various parts of the personality to the point that all of them, especially the conscious and the unconscious, begin to complement rather than oppose one another. The result is a self that is supra-ordinate even to the conscious ego.

During childhood one important aspect of development is the internalization of parental messages concerning the morality of behavior. Within this internalization process faith is also taken in from both parents and the authority figures of the adult world. In the terms of 'Transactional Analysis', developed by Eric Berne (as noted on page 68), all this becomes our 'parent ego state'. Because it becomes a part of us we cannot totally get rid of it. What, however, we must do if we are to grow into independent maturity, or complete the process of 'individuation', is to modify it, or even transform it so that it is in harmony with our adult situation in the here and now of the world we actually live in. The synthetic-conventional stage of faith is one very similar to the development of the 'parent ego state' in that it is a process of internalization of beliefs, ideas and morals from an external authority. It differs from the childhood process in two vital ways.

Firstly, it involves the intellect in a more active, critical way, and can include the rejection of values internalized earlier in childhood. Although the process can be seen to have close similarities, the authority figures from which beliefs and values are internalized are personally selected ones, in a way parents and schoolteachers are not. This leads us to the second difference, which is that it is a key movement on from childhood, because it is in a much greater degree an act of individual choice for which the individual adult takes responsibility. At the time the transition is taking place it is felt to be a very adult and independent thing, but later on one comes to realize that this is a partial truth. It is in fact just one step on from childhood dependency, albeit a very crucial one. From this stage any growth onwards becomes part of the process of individuation which alone happens to be the way to a full maturity. It is also a 'road less traveled' because of its insecurity and discomfort.

9.2 Biblical illustrations

I happen to think that from a faith perspective the Bible, when considered as a whole, spells out this process. Moreover, I am of the view that the person who actually does it and demonstrates the way is Jesus Christ, the Jewish Messiah. I next refer to two passages of scripture which seem to reflect this, because they say something very perceptive about a whole process that can be observed in many texts concerned with the themes of Messiahship and of 'entering the Kingdom of Heaven', which are the key ones concerning faith.

Firstly, one from the Old Testament: Jeremiah, 31:29–34. This passage is a prophecy concerning God [Yahweh], what will happen when the Messiah comes. It says that in this future stage of faith people will not need to have beliefs and morals imposed upon them by external authorities, but faith will be written in their hearts. This means that faith will be so deeply internalized and integrated within that the people will have a natural inner desire to behave in a good way and relate well to each other. External moral codes and means of guidance will become redundant, for, at verse 34:

> There will be no further need for neighbor to try to teach neighbor, or brother to say to brother, "Learn to know Yahweh!" No, they will all know me, the least no less than the greatest – it is Yahweh who speaks.

Secondly, one from the New Testament: it is Luke 14:26, chosen here because of its reference to the need for a process of individuation to take place within a believer before he or she can enter expansively into a fullness of life being clearly encouraged by Jesus, and emerging from spiritual maturity. This is not an isolated text, but one containing a statement that fits in with the wider theme of faith and 'the Kingdom of Heaven' dominant within Christ's teaching, and thus important both for a full understanding of the Christian story and of faith development. These words of Jesus are:

> If any man comes to me without hating his father, mother, wife, children, brothers, sisters, yes and his own life too, he cannot be my disciple.

Many people find this a very hard saying. Some even sense that the text is a mistake, and that Jesus could not have said such words. Maybe all who speculate about this are stuck in an earlier stage of faith, usually synthetic-conventional, and are not yet ready or able to move on. So how should we understand this text?

In The Jerusalem Bible there is a footnote to this text, saying that this is a 'Hebraism', being an emphatic way of expressing total detachment. The root meaning of the Hebrew word 'hate' is to oppose, or push away. This describes a very important psychological process essential for the growth of a person into full maturity as an adult. The well-nurtured healthy child starts to do this with mother at the age of about two, or in some cases earlier. This is repeated at adolescence in a more vigorous way, but because this period of life is far short of maturity, other authority figures are adopted. This happens in the process of developing the synthetic-conventional faith package and would indicate that such a stage of faith is well short of the maturity required for full entry into the Kingdom of God, though one must emphasize that it is a very important stage on the way. For full entry into the Kingdom, into which Jesus calls his disciples, all authority figures as people to whom one has a strong attachment must be safely pushed away so that the faith held becomes totally one's own, coming from within one's own being. This is the nature and outcome of a fully 'individuated' person. The individuative-reflective stage of faith is the beginning of this process whereby we enter the Kingdom on our own independent volition. I see this text as one that focuses much of the whole of the message of Jesus. Let me now give a few examples of this.

In the Gospel story the main opponents of Jesus were the Pharisees. These people were the regional religious representatives of the current synthetic-conventional faith package into which Jesus was born and nurtured. He seems to be encouraging people to move beyond it, but never does he despise it. He just demonstrates its inadequacies (see Matthew's Gospel, chapter 23). Because Jesus did this the Pharisees as a body behaved in the standard defensive way of those stuck in the synthetic-conventional stage, which in the end led them to plot his mock trial and crucifixion.

In St. John's Gospel, chapter 3, we see one of the Pharisees, Nicodemus, coming for secret talks with Jesus. This I believe was to do with his being aware of his own need to move on faithwise, but being afraid of the reactions of his Pharisee colleagues if he did so openly. I see this as an example of the pain people have who do move on from their synthetic-conventional stage, caused by the powerful and often violent reaction from those they leave behind.

Many of Jesus' parables point out the danger of getting stuck in the synthetic-conventional stage. In the parable of the Good Samaritan the priest and Levite, maintainers of the current synthetic-conventional faith, do not come out as the heroes of the story. The parable of the sheep and goats (St. Matthew, 25:31 to end) I see as a very solemn warning to those stuck at the synthetic-conventional stage. I do so because it can become a spiritually complacent stage in which one feels safe, comfortable, and to have arrived!

As a third instance, I cite St. Paul as an example of one who went through the transition from synthetic-conventional to individuative-reflective stage, and no doubt beyond. His dramatic conversion from Pharisee to Christian, his personal history and his writings all reflect this. I do not think it appropriate to go through this in detail, but mention one passage of his writings which I believe show this to be the case. It is as recorded within his first letter to the Corinthians, 3:11–15:

> For the foundation, nobody can lay any other than the one which has already been laid, that is Jesus Christ. On this foundation you can build in gold, silver and jewels, or in wood, grass and straw, but whatever the material, the work of each builder is going to be clearly revealed when the day comes. That day will begin with fire, and the fire will test the

> quality of each man's work. If his structure stands up to it, he will get his wages; if it is burnt down, he will be the loser, and though he is saved himself, it will be as one who has gone through the fire.

I understand this passage in terms of personal spiritual growth. It is seen by Paul as being essential for our total fulfillment within God's kingdom. He sees Jesus Christ as the originator and enabler of his process, but he also sees that, among all those who decide to be disciples of Jesus within God's kingdom, many will not develop their faith in such a way as to get all the benefits possible. Implied is that many will stick at the synthetic-conventional stage because it is either more comfortable to do so, or that they do not have the energy or courage to go through the pain of moving on. Fear can so grip a person that they become paralyzed and stay where they are. The sad thing is that many people to whom we have become attached, and who themselves are still at the synthetic-conventional stage can have enormous power over us, and because our struggle to move on will threaten them they can easily become our persecutors and accusers.

I have just used scriptural examples to illustrate how movement from synthetic-conventional to individuative-reflective faith comes about. However, it is my opinion that developmental patterns and processes that can be observed in scripture are universal. We see them repeated throughout history and in our everyday existence now. May I cite as an example an article written in *The Tablet*, 9th Nov 1996, by former medical missionary Dr. Anne Townsend called 'Out of the Playpen' as a graphic description of one person's move from the synthetic-conventional to the individuative-reflective stage. She describes (and more fully in her 1990 book *Faith without Pretending*) how for years she held a fundamentalist evangelical form of the Christian Faith. As she entered middle age certain painful experiences shook the certainties of this form of faith and she went through a very traumatic period of breakdown. Things she had been taught up to that point did not equip her to cope with life as she now experienced it.

I find it interesting that the cause of Anne's questioning was to do with death, pain and suffering. She had held a very naive and childish belief as part of the synthetic-conventional faith package that God would protect those who believed in Him from very painful things. This belief is one that can only be held within a very controlling group structure. Such is in fact in total opposition to the Gospel and to the history of the life of Jesus and the early Church. It is always an inadequate faith and yet many cling to it, not only evangelical fundamentalists but many others such as rigid Catholics of various types, Anglo and Roman, as well as humanists, materialists, evolutionists, and a wide variety of other belief systems. Faith based on a very well-defined and narrow doctrinal principle, re-enforced by rigorous intellectual means, will always come a cropper upon the rocks of death, pain, suffering, and anything else our day-to-day experience of life should confront us with that we find unpalatable, *unless* it has a deeper, non intellectual and spiritually durable element within it.

It seems to me, from what Anne Townsend wrote, that within her synthetic-conventional faith package this extra dimension was present and with the help of a chaplain who was further along the road of faith, she was enabled to move on to a greater maturity of faith herself. I have found in my counseling work that those who can't, at an appropriate time in their lives, move beyond the synthetic-conventional stage of faith, or who reject everything to do with this stage, were very inadequately nurtured at some earlier stage of their development. I see it as being a fact that we all need to go through this stage, so the practical issue is about providing wise guidance both to those at this stage and to those moving out of it, rather than having a condemnatory attitude. My only possible criticism of this article is that it contained an undercurrent of criticism rather than an accepting attitude which said, 'That's how things are and this is how I worked my way through it.' I would now like to quote the last two paragraphs of this article because they are a very good description of the positive transition from synthetic-conventional to an individuative-reflective faith.

> I now realize from many people who have contacted me in recent years that I am but one of many hundreds of Evangelical Christians from the more fundamentalist end of evangelicalism who have recently accepted the terror, isolation and guilt of moving away from their familiar religious pathways. Now we journey through new territory – barren deserts and lush, formerly forbidden, green pastures. We have discovered in a deeper way how our Shepherd leads us.
>
> As I approach the age of three score years, I am grateful to have left the spiritual 'playpen' in which I barricaded myself away for a large part of my life.

The only comment I wish to add is that the words 'fundamentalist' and 'evangelical' could be replaced by many other words that describe a wide variety of faiths lived at the synthetic-conventional level, so not seen as a basic criticism of evangelicalism *per se*. What Anne says is to do with psychological and spiritual development, and not the intrinsic value of any particular doctrinal understanding. Evangelicals can mature beyond the synthetic-conventional stage and still remain basically evangelical, as also can those holding other doctrinal expressions of faith.

9.3 Some conclusions concerning this individuative-reflective stage of faith

The main conclusion one can draw from what we know of this

stage of faith is that it is a very vulnerable one. Those who are in it have moved on from being cocooned in the certainties of the synthetic-conventional, with all its support systems and other ways of re-enforcement, into a stage that can be very lonely. It also can make those in it appear to be too individualistic and difficult in the eyes of anyone still happily at home in a previous stage of growth. The simple truth is that that is how things are and how they should be accepted, welcoming rooted change as people grow. Unfortunately there are far too many insecure people in the world who cannot behave in this way, so that when they feel threatened all too easily they become dogmatic and defensive. Those unable to grasp the individuative-reflective stage view those who do as awkward, intellectually difficult backsliders, or apostates. The person at this stage can react and see themselves as being intellectually superior and not in need of religious props. In reflecting on these facts and also remembering the time when I was going through this stage, I make the following final points.

i) *The danger of 'throwing the baby out with the bath water'*

This is a very real danger at this stage, especially with people whose synthetic-conventional faith package is weak in intellectual content. Because the intellect is dominant at this stage it can be used negatively to suppress threatening emotions that underlie it. It is at the next stage of faith development that these emotions are integrated as individuation is completed; but at this stage they cannot be adequately dealt with because the intellectual framework within which this can happen successfully is not in place. The task at this stage is to put it in place, calling for skilled support from one who has completed their own individuation process and become stabilized at the next stage of faith. I find it a sad fact that within contemporary cultural mores there are too few such people available.

People who stick at this stage and 'throw out the baby with

the bath water' go round and round in circles discussing everything at length but coming to no definite conclusion. They avoid anything with emotional content and condemn it as immature. They cannot make commitments and become very cynical about those at the synthetic-conventional stage, seeing nothing at all positive in it, and often being threatened by people at that stage of faith development. I believe such people to be victims of earlier inadequate faith nurture and in need of some very stable, mature and wise support if they are to come through it and re-establish themselves in a viable and sound faith. In the whole of life, sound early nurture gives us something to be treasured, for it is often only in later life that the negative results of the converse appear. Healing is then a very painful process, even at times too painful to be undertaken.

ii) *The importance of strong supportive structures*

The kind of social structures within which people can be supported as they enter into and move through the individuative-reflective stage of faith need to be very strong, tolerant (I use this word in its strictest meaning which is 'able to bear heavy burdens without collapsing'), and insightful as to what is going on in such people. Sadly my observation is that most faith communities do not have such structures. As a result such people are made into outsiders, or if they are strong and resourceful create new communities which also tend to disintegrate simply because a person at this stage of faith does not have the stability to lead a new faith community. They only, in fact, form a personal support club that is an understandable thing to do when one is lonely and in a state of transition.

The reason for this problem is that faith communities and institutions seem to be predominantly stuck at the synthetic-conventional stage, and therefore are strongly motivated to keep everyone at this stage because of the threat presented by those moving on, and the congregational inability to understand them.

The structures must be truly 'catholic' and strong enough in mature faith to contain, absorb and develop faith in individuals. In such circumstances people can grow and develop without either rejecting all that has gone before, or being rejected by institutions from which they desperately need nurturing support. I use the word 'catholic' in the sense of it expressing something of a universal, mature, and very stable nature, in which all expressions of individual need can be contained, nurtured, developed and integrated. Often I meet people who say they are 'catholic' of one sort or another and find that they are using the word merely as a description of their brand of synthetic-conventional faith. I would apply this to very extreme Anglo-Catholics and a great deal of dogma that comes out of the Vatican.

I am aware that this point raises an issue on which much debate can be based. But it is an illustration of the issues that come up at this stage of faith development.

iii) *The vulnerability of those at this stage of faith development*

What makes this stage so vulnerable is its very nature. It is because it is predominantly intellectual. When one has worked out an intellectual framework of faith which appears on the surface to be satisfying, this stage appears to have been completed. There is a sense in which it has, but the reality is that all that has been completed is the establishment of an intellectual framework from which it is possible to deal with the inner traumas of moving into the next stage.

In short, this stage of faith marks only the beginning of the individuation process, and the next sixth stage completes it. To stick at this fifth stage is to become 'half-baked' and very easily threatened. To move on can be very painful but in the end satisfying. It is an emotional-cum-faith reflection of our physical birth. We are at the threshold of the possibility of entering a new world. At this stage the material of the subconscious has not been tapped or even seriously entered. As a result, there will come a time when intellectual 'certainties' are threatened by the unexpected entrance into the conscious mind of the irrational, which cannot be avoided or explained away. The only viable option is to embrace these things and integrate them into one's faith structures. When this happens, the next sixth stage of faith development has begun and can continue for a long time.

Chapter 10

Stage 6 – The Conjunctive Stage of Faith Development

The word 'conjunctive' means that which joins together separate entities to make a greater and more functional whole. An example of this is the human body. Tissues that join together bones and muscles are called conjunctive tissues. They are very important parts of the body because without them the body could not function as a harmonious whole and efficient unit. Human personality is much more complex and difficult to define than the physical body.

Much of human personality is a mystery, and those of us who have spent a lifetime trying to understand human behavior have to admit in the end that there are always cases that baffle us. Because of this one is often left feeling lost, inadequate and not in control. The natural response to this is to seek intellectual definitions of those troublesome irrational and out of control aspects that threaten us; and from this point we are so easily driven into reductionism. Reductionism then excludes certain things in order to make everything look rational and under control. We then end up in denial of the unruly elements within the human personality that are essential for our wholeness or completion as a fully human being.

In brief, it can be said that the intellectual part of us is the controllable and non-threatening bit; the emotional, the uncontrollable but threatening bit. Both are parts of the whole and must be recognized as such. In the analogy of the physical body both bones and muscles are part of the whole. In this body conjunctive tissue joins together bone and muscle as a functioning unit. So it is also in the case of faith development in the human personality, the conjunctive stage being a process by which the intellectual and emotional elements of faith are joined and reconciled. This is the second part of Jung's process of 'individuation', when personality's 'bone and muscle' is joined creatively together within the 'structural skeleton' developed in the previous stages of development of faith.

The process by which a person grows into conjunctive faith can be a very painful one. That is why this transition comes mostly at a late stage of a normal life-cycle, because to make it possible all the previous stages need to be well set in place as foundations. Much of its outworking involves plunging into the depths of the unconscious, and this requires the confidence to be able to remain adrift and lost in a sea of inner turmoil and unfamiliar emotions for long periods of time, without any understanding at all of where we are.

The Old Testament prophet Job echoes this situation in the statement: *'Though He slay me, yet will I serve Him'*. I see this as an essentially simple statement saying clearly that when Job was pitched into his pain and turmoil he had already established a sound faith foundation that would enable him to come into an eventual stronger state of faith. I see the Book of Job as a statement about the outworking of this sixth stage of faith. Those who do not have the foundation of having worked through the previous stages are likely to find Job's book confusing and so misunderstand it. Having stated what this stage is about, let us now develop what has been said by use of examples, beginning with the Book of Job.

10.1 The example of Job

In the book of Job it can be said that we have a drama about faith, with a cast of seven actors. The actors are: God (the object of faith), the devil (who is the accuser and tester of the faithful person), Job (the man of faith), and finally the four comforters who try to help Job, but fail because their faith position is not adequate enough.

This drama is full of symbolism and mystery, but it makes a point that is valid universally and at all times about the nature of faith. It is that *the basis of faith is relationship, and not dogma or any form of intellectually verifiable belief system*. Where this relationship exists, even in an undeveloped form, it will never be destroyed. Indeed it will grow, develop and be strengthened by adversity. Any belief system that attempts to express intellectually this basic faith will be able to be modified by negative and harsh experience, but will never be destroyed. The experiences of the Nazi Holocaust in our times are an example of this, affirming the message of the Book of Job. I quote from *Journey Back from Hell* by Anton Gill:

> As with many survivors... the degree of his religious faith was not affected by the concentration camp experience... Those who did believe before the camps in general continued to; those who were mildly or conventionally religious quite frequently lost their faith.

In the drama of Job, his unjust sufferings did not destroy his faith at all; indeed they strengthened and developed it. In faith development terms he grew through them from the starting point of being synthetic-conventional through the individuative-reflective into the conjunctive stage, and quite possibly beyond. How far beyond will emerge later in this chapter.

The Job drama is very Jewish. Having seven characters is indicative of this. The Jewish mindset would see the symbolism of seven as representing completion, for the Genesis poem of creation sees God completing His creative work in seven days or 'stages of development'. This symbolism also expresses another aspect of the Old Testament which is that on the surface it may seem exclusively for the Jews, but its deeper spiritual implications are actually universal for all people at all times. It is like a spiritual time bomb that exploded on the whole world with the coming of Jesus Christ, and truly a paradigm of real faith.

When the genuine seed is sown in the depths of a person's being it goes on growing and growing, becoming more and more universal and all encompassing. The mystery is in the paradox of two opposites. It has to be very exclusive in order to become truly inclusive. It also has to be inward and deeply personal, perhaps a little selfishly navel gazing, before it can get to the stage of going outward in love to others. We see all this in the drama of Job, and we also see this in faith development. Job's arrival at the synthetic-conventional stage had obviously come about through an adequate nurture that had sown in him a sound seed of faith which enabled him to move on. One wonders about Job's comforters, but now let us move through the drama.

10.2 The drama of Job

Act I: The Opening Scene

On earth Job is a happy man. He is well established in material terms and is respected for his faith and godliness. He is at the synthetic-conventional stage of faith and so are all his friends and admirers.

In heaven God is holding court when along comes Satan, the accuser, and challenges God to let him try to destroy Job's faith. God says OK, get on with it. Do as you wish but don't destroy his personality, meaning 'Keep your hands off his person'. So Satan does as God has permitted. Job gets in a terrible state as a result of this. He is in dispute with God, says he is innocent, challenges all the beliefs of his received synthetic-conventional faith in which he has been nurtured, but does not reject God. His disputing with God is so open and vigorous that his friends come, initially, to comfort, but when this fails to reprove…

Act II: The Dialogue

This opens with Job's initial statement. In it he makes the

following points:

i) My condition is so bad that there is no hope. I might as well be dead.
ii) This is all unjust and arbitrary. There is no reason at all why this disaster should fall on me. Nothing makes any sense.
iii) God is just a despot and tyrant to do this. By having faith in Him one gains nothing. Just as in nature, the beasts attack and devour each other, so it is in the human realm. Human beings count little in this world; they are just a part of nature, always vulnerable to its arbitrary and unpredictable moods. God does not treat His friends very well.

These points are a very standard human response to suffering disaster and tragedy. I have heard all this so often in my years of ministry and counseling. It is the standard cry of the afflicted human soul. However, the next two complaints are not quite as common.

iv) 'I am innocent'. Job makes this protest consistently and with great confidence. Most people, in my experience, who attempt to assert their innocence do so hesitantly and generally tinged with guilt. Here Job is not giving a run of the mill response, and the assertion of his innocence, so vigorously made, is associated with the fact that at no time does he deny God. There would appear to be an underlying confidence in Job that enables him, as it were, to take God on in dispute with no holds barred, neither denying his existence nor feebly giving in to Him in an act of submissive piety.
v) 'Whatever I fear comes true, whatever I dread befalls me' (chapter 3, verse 25). This statement is interesting because

> it is the voice of the unconscious. It shows that Job has a degree of contact with his inner self, which is a healthy thing.

As Carl Jung clearly pointed out, *our unconscious never lies* whereas our intellect sometimes does, and when it does it can cleverly deceive us. The agenda of those entering the conjunctive stage of faith development is about hearing and coming to terms with those disquieting voices from the unconscious. They are disquieting because they come from our pre-verbal stages of life and tell us of infantile pain that has been coped with for years by a process of vigorous repression. More will be said of this later, but at this stage it is just noted to show that early on in the dialogue Job showed an emotional maturity and soundness of faith nurture earlier in life. This would give him a confidence to battle it out with God, and by so doing be enabled to progress rather than regress and totally lose faith. His comforters failed him because they did not have this and were as a result very threatened by Job's protests. We now turn to their responses, beginning with Eliphaz.

The response of Eliphaz to Job's sufferings could be called 'The appeal to common sense.' Its general tone is:

> 'Come off it, Job, old chap. Just think honestly about your life history. You have done well, you are respected, you have helped others and made a name for yourself. All this must count for something, so don't get yourself into such a state. Take it all on the chin like the man you are. You will get over it in the end; and don't give in to bad emotions like anger. That won't get you anywhere.'

In his three speeches Eliphaz makes the following points:

The First Speech

i) Have confidence in your past achievements and don't just moan about your present negative situation.
ii) Look on the bright side. The righteous never suffer for long; therefore it will soon be all over.
iii) Nobody is perfect, not even the good and great like you. Just accept it all and ask God to help; but don't get angry with Him.

The Second Speech

In this speech Eliphaz begins to show his frustration because all his common sense reasoning seems to have achieved nothing. He just re-emphasizes the points he has already made and 'pulls rank' on Job by saying, 'I am mature and wise. I know what I am talking about, so you had better take notice.'

The Third Speech

Eliphaz is by this time very angry with Job. He simply tells Job that he is so belligerent and negative that he has called down God's punishment on himself and that is that. Having made this point he gives up and leaves.

In response to all this, Job makes two simple points:

i) He has heard all such religious claptrap before and is bored with it.
ii) It is all too simplistic and does not take fully into account all the facts which are: Firstly, God has gone far away from Job and evil has triumphed; and secondly, Job is being honest and throughout he has kept his own integrity before God.

The First Speech of Bildad

In the first of his three speeches Bildad sets out the basis of his approach to Job's sufferings. It is one so commonly used today by moral theologians, and in my opinion, is a standard one for all whose faith expression is firmly set at the synthetic-conventional stage of development. It is based on law and logic and is very straightforward. It is like this: if you are suffering it is because you have sinned. Find out what your besetting sin is and confess it, then you will be forgiven and healed, and your suffering will cease.

Job's reply to this is quite simply that God's justice is above law. Just as Eliphaz's appeal to common sense does not answer his cry for help, neither does this legal argument, no matter how soundly logical it might appear. It is simplistic and takes no account of the great mystery of suffering; neither does it give any relief or comfort to the sufferer. Job feels deeply within himself that it makes no difference at all whether the sufferer is innocent or guilty of sin. The suffering is just the same!

The Second Speech

In this speech Bildad dwells upon the evil of anger. He says it is a futile thing at best, and at worst it is destructive.

Job's response to this is that throughout it all he has been completely faithful, even though God has deserted him. In this speech comes the very well-known statement of faith, 'I know that my redeemer lives,' (chapter 19, verses 25–27). This is an expression of Job's belief that in the end all will be well and shows how he is moving on in faith far beyond his comforters.

The Third Speech

In this speech Bildad does not know what to say in view of Job's previous responses. He appears to be defeated. All he can say is that God is great, wonderful and perfect. Therefore He must never be challenged as Job is doing.

Job replies that everything Bildad has said is empty and meaningless because Job knows he is innocent. At this point Bildad gives up and leaves.

The Speeches of Zophar

It is obvious that Zophar is unable to cope with the torrent of words coming from Job. His anger and the power of the emotions are just too much. In short, the message of Zophar is: 'Just shut up and admit your sin and stop causing us embarrassment and trouble.'

The First Speech

In this speech Zophar makes the following points:

i) The mysteries of God's dealings with us are such that we can only accept them without question.
ii) The only way to live a good life is passive acceptance of this and by doing so we obtain comfort.

Job's reply to this is as follows:

i) I accept that the ways of God are a mystery, but this is best seen in God's dreadful works of omnipotence which always leaves man powerless and looking foolish.
ii) This very point is justification enough for us to protest, therefore I shall continue with mine.
iii) You, Zophar, have a cheek in telling me what I already know. My dispute is with God and human advice is not relevant.

The Second Speech

In this exchange the following points are made:

> Job is not special in his relationship with God. Justice is impersonal and Job is getting his just reward for daring to assume a special relationship with God.

This view is totally rejected by Job on the grounds that it does not fit the facts of life as he has experienced them.

The Third Speech

This speech makes one more point. Zophar simply says, Job you are not only a hopeless case but you are also accursed. It is simple logic that if a person suffers it must be because they are wicked. Job is plainly avoiding the issue and therefore he is most certainly accursed.

Job does not reply to this and Zophar leaves.

At this point is inserted a hymn in praise of wisdom. It is not attributed to anyone and says that wisdom is beyond man's reach. Only God has it. Psalm 73, verses 15 to 18 seems to give an answer to the questions raised at the end of this hymn, which is that unless God chooses to reveal wisdom to man, man must remain ignorant.

At this point Job is left alone and makes a speech that sums up all that has been said to him by the three presumed 'comforters', who have given up on him and left the scene. Here Job makes the following three points:

i) He recalls his former happiness and lifestyle. As he reflects on this he says that during this time he believed totally that he was secure and happy, nothing terrible could ever happen to him. This blessed lifestyle would continue until he died because he was a righteous man.

ii) Next he describes his present misery. Everything he had ever hoped for had been destroyed and taken away. Two points he makes very strongly: they are that he is totally innocent; and during his time of suffering, God has remained totally silent.

iii) He ends by listing everything that he has ever done and thought. As he does so he points to the fact that none of this would be evidence of any wrongdoing on his part, and he does not deserve punishment. The conclusion of the speech is a statement that he is very confident in his standing before God, that it is good. He has no fear of condemnation and demands a hearing from God.

The Speech of Elihu

This final speech of the human dialogue comes out of the silence after Job had finished. It has the form of a long monologue. In it Elihu makes the following points in addition to repeating much that has been said before:

i) He is a young man and therefore listened in the background when his elders and betters tried to sort Job out.
ii) As an enthusiastic young man the other three old wise men made him very angry because they had failed to sort Job out and had let God down. He was forced against his better judgment to say something to put this dismal failure right.
iii) All that has been said already is repeated in Elihu's own particular way, and the speech ends with a song of praise to God and advice to Job that he should now go away and meditate upon the truths that had been so forcefully put before him.

Job makes no response at all to the speech of Elihu. One gets the sense that all human activity has ceased and we are left with a marked silence in which it is possible for God to speak.

Act III: The Conclusion

This final part of the story is the dialogue between Job and God. Now at last Job gets what he has been asking God for. He has an intimate, face-to-face relationship with Him, that is, in as far as one can have such a relationship with God. In the silence God is first to speak. It would seem that for man to be in a position to hear God speak he must first get himself into a position of quietness or inner silence. This is not easy and takes time. It is a process that each person must go through in whatever way is relevant for them. Events in one's life and the process of dialogue with other people can be that which stimulates this process, as was the case with Job. This, however, is not all that is required. We need as well to be in touch with our inner selves, and have laid within us a seed of faith that is fertile. Job seems to have had this also. Let us now return to the dialogue between God and Job.

God Speaks

i) God tells Job that he must bow to the Creator's wisdom, and not to man or even man's interpretation of God. Chapters 38 and 39 put forward the argument that man is not capable of knowing many things, and especially the things of God. They are a mystery too great for him, and only to be known if and when God chooses to reveal them. God here takes the initiative and acts in the process of revelation, and man must learn to respond to this. This is the basis of what the Eastern Orthodox theologians call 'apophatic' or negative theology. It is that God can only be defined by statements about what he is not. This is so because God is greater than us, and science and the human intellect can only analyze and understand those things that are limited and smaller than man. Understanding God and suffering does not come from intellectual activity. There is a sense in which the message of Job points us to Jesus Christ, who in his incarnation was the fullest possible revelation of God to man. The historical incarnate man Jesus reveals God to us in his life, suffering, death and resurrection, but in so doing remains man and directs us to something more in ways that we can grasp. The understanding of Jesus comes not by a process of intellectual wrestling, but through a process of relating, waiting, praying and perceiving. We have to 'Walk with him on our life's journey, and on the walk He will reveal himself to us.' This is the 'Road to Emmaus experience' recorded in St. Luke's Gospel 24:13–35).

ii) Job gives in to God in a way he could not do so to the arguments of man. Something in him recognized the authenticity of God's voice. This surrender allows Job to listen for God to say more to him.

iii) Now God continues because Job is in the right attitude to hear.

God begins by telling Job to 'Brace himself as a fighter', because he will have to wrestle with what is about to be shown him. This to me has echoes of the term 'Swink and sweat' used in the famed *Cloud of Unknowing* as a description of what those who desire a mystical experience of God must go through before they can receive it. God makes the following points to Job:

a) God controls all the forces of evil.

b) God uses these forces for the purpose of testing His faithful servants in order to develop their faith.

c) When suffering, human beings must trust, and allow the suffering and evil to work its purpose out. It is futile to ask why and expect a rational explanation.

d) It is a good thing for a sufferer to protest to God and dispute as Job did. It is more valid to challenge God than to avoid conflict with Him. In the end it is the relationship man has with God that is important. Without this relationship in the first place it becomes impossible to grow through suffering.

Job's final response to God is adequately summed up in chapter 42, verses 5 and 6:

> I knew you then only by hearsay; but now having seen you with my own eyes, I retract all I have said, and in dust and ashes I repent.

This shows clearly that, as a result of his sufferings, Job had moved on from synthetic-conventional faith through individuative-reflective to conjunctive. Knowing by hearsay is what happens in synthetic-conventional faith. The group is very powerful in forming the belief system, and equally so in making sure its members do not depart from it. Individuative-reflective development is the disputing stage which Job did well. At the same time his comforters tried to keep him within the synthetic-conventional group to which they had all belonged before Job's tragedy.

In the course of all this Job moves well into a conjunctive stage which is indicated by his direct awareness of God, and coming to a place of peace within himself. There are two important factors that enabled Job to thus develop in faith. Firstly, that he must have had a well-laid basic foundation of trust in the early childhood stages of faith; and secondly, that his sufferings were the main stimulus to this growth in faith. Both are essential in the development of a really mature faith.

In going through the pain of his sufferings and keeping his own integrity Job ends up with even greater blessings, as do all who have the courage to work out the painful agenda that entering the conjunctive stage of faith demands.

Having dealt with Job and seen him arrive at a sound state of faith, God reprimands Eliphaz, Bildad and Zophar because they had not spoken truthfully of Him as Job had done. He also says that they must do a penance and Job will pray for them. God will listen to Job's prayers, and as a result He will excuse their folly. It would seem that the three comforters were stuck in a state of faith far behind where they should be, and now Job, who had grown beyond them, was able to become the agent of their growth. Young Elihu was left out of doing penance, even though what he said to Job was at the same level as the other three. It would seem that the reason for this was because he was young and his behavior was what one would expect. He was at a stage of faith development appropriate to his age, whereas the other three were not.

A lot of space has been given here to Job because I see him as the archetypal example of growth into conjunctive faith. I would like to refer briefly to a few others, and then end with my own experience, as one who is well into this stage of spiritual development, but not yet beyond it.

10.3 Other examples of this stage transition

The first further example is St. Augustine of Hippo. His spiritual journey is well recorded in *The Confessions*. As a child he was nurtured in the Christian Faith and then as a young man at the synthetic-conventional stage, but rejected it during the individuative-reflective stage. Eventually, through quite a dramatic conversion he came back to a fuller faith during the conjunctive stage. Whereas *The Confessions* dwells mainly on the emotional turmoil of the conjunctive stage, all through it one can see clear references to all previous stages, especially the nurture given by his mother, and some of the most graphic stories he relates are to do with childhood experiences. His experiences as a Manichean during the individuative-reflective stage show how people try out all kinds of things that are contrary to their previous faith nurture in order to test them out, especially if there is something slightly inadequate at childhood stages of nurture. We know that in Augustine's case there was. I see the evidence we have as pointing to a very dominant mother and an unavailable, inadequate father. In Augustine's other main work, *City of God*, we have evidence of the other important factor in faith development. It is that unless a person finds faith in the experiential reality of a relationship with a God who is both transcendent, that is above and beyond us, but at the same time immanent and available to us where we are, faith cannot develop to this stage. It tends to get stuck either at the synthetic-conventional, or at the individuative-reflective stage. Sticking in either of these stages does not give a person inner peace. In the former, one becomes aggressively defensive of the faith group within which one is stuck, and in the later one lives in a state of permanent anxiety or angst so typical of many intellectuals in 'post modern' society.

The second further example is J.R.R. Tolkien, who, importantly, was instrumental in inspiring C.S. Lewis, of whom more next. The reason for this ability to inspire lay in the fact that Tolkien's expression of his Christian faith had matured well into the conjunctive stage. He was thus able to integrate the emotional and imaginative with the intellectual aspects of faith. At this time C.S. Lewis could not. An outcome of Tolkien's conjunctive faith was his theory of 'sub-creation'. The theory was that when mankind draws things from God's world and creates his own world, he is acting as a sub-creator. In this theory, creativity is the prerogative of God alone, and is thus the basis of everything that happens. Therefore, intellect, imagination and emotion are all equally valid and must be employed in harmony without any one predominating. This integrating factor Tolkien expressed is evidence of conjunctive faith. It enabled C.S. Lewis to move on and integrate his intellect with his imagination. It was the outcome of a good relationship between the two men; and, as we have seen in the example of Job, faith, like our very existence, is very dependent upon relationships.

C.S. Lewis rejected the faith in which he had been nurtured at the beginning of the synthetic-conventional stage of development when he was about 14 years old. The problem for him was that it did not seem reasonable. He could not make sense of it in relationship to his experience of life. A few years later he was in the trenches, seeing the stupidity of war and its suffering. This no doubt would re-enforce his rejection of faith in a loving God. As the years of youth and early manhood passed, he became very militantly atheistic, disputing on the basis of reason alone that God did not exist and faith in Him was nonsense. I see in this period of his life an entry into the individuative-reflective stage. The evidence of this is the vigorous intellectual activity into which he enthusiastically entered, the main indication that a person is in this stage of faith development. The outcome of this debating stage was that he came to see the Christian Faith as being reasonable, as having intellectual validity; and it was at this point, at the end of the individuative-reflective period, that he formed a friendship with J.R.R. Tolkien.

It would seem to me that Tolkien was just the sort of man to help him into the conjunctive stage. The biggest barrier to a developed faith appears to have been Lewis's inability to reconcile reason and imagination. Until this phase, reason had suppressed imagination as a dangerous and threatening inner demon that could lead one astray. Tolkien helped Lewis to be truly conjunctive integrating them both into a more wholesome, balanced personality. Lewis then saw reason as being 'the organ of truth' and imagination 'the organ of meaning.' All his subsequent works show how he had integrated these two into a dynamic living and growing faith. Imagination was in him all the time, but not earlier valued as an equal partner with intellect.

I think that the power of all Lewis's writings about the Christian Faith is due to the fact that they were written by a man who had matured into a balanced fullness of faith through and beyond the conjunctive stage. He not only came to terms with the threatening bits of himself, which had been denied at an earlier stage, but he integrated them into a healthy wholeness of being. When questioned about his use of imagination in his writing, Lewis once spoke of there being 'a guiding thread. The imaginative man in me is older, more continuously operative, and in that sense more basic than either the religious writer or critic.' A mark of having fully arrived at this conjunctive stage of faith is the ability to do this, know one is doing it, and be very comfortable with it, as Lewis indeed was for the later, most creative part of his life.

10.4 Summarizing remarks

This sixth stage of faith can last a very long time. There are important issues that face those within it. Central is the need for support from someone who has sufficient understanding. This means one who is well into this stage themselves and has learned to live inside it. Not one of Job's comforters was qualified because they were all at the synthetic-conventional stage. All that they said was irrelevant because they had no experience of the key issues involved, which are:

a) The ability to live comfortably with paradox and to understand its nature. Paradox is about two apparently conflicting concepts both being equally true, both being expressions of a greater truth that is beyond our present understanding.
b) The ability to live for an indefinite period with uncomfortable and even painful emotions without projecting them onto other people or situations as a means of easing the pain by a process of rationalization. In practical terms this is about the ability to live one day at a time in situations that do not make sense or have any known resolution, and at the same time retain a sense of inner peace and dignity.
c) To have matured well beyond being concerned about one's personal image. How other people perceive those who are at this stage of faith matters very little to them. At earlier stages, and especially at the synthetic-conventional, it matters a lot. Being 'sound' is a very key issue then, but means little now. Job showed this in his attitude to his comforters who made the basis of their appeal to

him from within the safe boundaries of this earlier stage.

d) It is impossible to develop one's faith as far as this stage if the object of faith is not spiritual and so largely outside and beyond the material world. For example, those whose belief system is based totally upon science, political or social theory, or anything that does not take account of a spiritual world outside our present material existence, will not be able to enter this stage of faith development.

An interesting down-to-earth and practical example of this is seen in the methods of Alcoholics Anonymous. Its twelve steps involve an admission of being powerless to cope with problems involved in being alcoholic, together with the need to rely on 'A Higher Power'. The Higher Power is to me obviously God, but too many have had their understanding of God so destroyed by bad religion that it needs to be expressed in this way. Nevertheless AA works because it points to an essential aspect of being. That for completeness and human fulfillment, relationship with the transcendent is essential. At this stage of faith people begin the process of entering into this relationship by the dual process of living in their weakness, whatever that might be, and making spiritual contact, involving the whole person, with God who is beyond and as far as human effort alone is concerned, unknowable.

As Jung's process of individuation is completed this stage of faith comes to its conclusion and the person is able to move on to the next and final stage. This movement is slower than the movement between previous stages, being one of slow evolution. Long before this stage is completed people can experience being in the next one for a short time and then slip back. This is especially so in the case of those who have become well practiced in the art of contemplative prayer, even though for most of the time it is a struggle. It seems essential to make the effort in understanding and practicing contemplation for faith to develop in any way during the later stages of our lives. Not to do so risks getting stuck at earlier stages.

Chapter 11

Stage 7 – The Final Stage of Universalizing Faith

JW Fowler does not say as much about this seventh stage as he does the other stages. The reason being that so few people reach it, and therefore there is a lack of material for objective study. It is also a stage in our life in which developmental psychologists have so far shown little interest. In his book, *Faith Development and Pastoral Care,* Fowler sees those entering this stage as moving beyond the paradoxical awareness and the embrace of the polar tensions of the conjunctive stage. Thus on page 75 we read:

> With those persons who are drawn beyond the Conjunctive into the Universalizing stage of faith, we seem to see a movement in which the self is drawn beyond itself into a new quality of participation and grounding in God, or the principle of Being.

From this starting point I wish to enlarge upon this statement of Fowler's, which I think is true and very accurately stated, by looking at some of the works of mystics from the past, and reflecting upon my own experience. In using the term, 'my own experience', I do not mean just my personal spiritual life, but also my experience of other people with whom I have had a close relationship. I believe that more people than those recognized by Fowler enter some degree of Universalizing Faith near the end of their lives. They are what could be described as 'ordinary people'; those who get on quietly with their lives but do not leave records, written in diaries, or autobiographies. They are those whom, to quote Ecclesiasticus, 'Have perished as though they have never been'. These are the people pastors meet in the daily round of their ministry, and there are many of them.

Another important observation I have made from my own experience is that for such people, Universalizing Faith is very rarely a state into which they enter permanently. It is one into which they enter on some days and regress from, back into Conjunctive Faith, on others. This movement is something that happens that cannot be controlled. It would seem to me to be part of a larger ongoing process that is a part of human history, larger than the individual but its nature is such that every individual is caught up in it in a way peculiar to each individual. The choice an individual has is either to recognize it and go with it, or to deny it and resist it. Having painted the broader picture, I will now further develop it by use of examples.

11.1 Biblical examples

Before choosing several specific examples by way of illustration, I would like to emphasize a few general comments about the Bible. As previously noted (page 62), the Bible is not just a book, but a collection of books of various kinds covering several thousand years of history, and includes the experiences of many people. These experiences are often, but not always, faith experiences in which both groups and individuals demonstrate how they experience God in a living relationship with Him. It is obvious that these experiences of God are all interpreted by these groups and individuals in the light of their own personalities and where they happen to be in historical terms. We see in it many things common to all human beings. Goodness, wickedness, strength, frailty, courage, fear, and so on – just about everything human beings can experience, often very graphically described either in story form, poetry, or plain historical fact. This then is the Bible in all its many facets.

The second point about the Bible is that its message concerning faith is progressive and evolutionary. It develops through stages that can be recognized and this culminates and focuses in the person of Jesus Christ who is the central figure of both Old and New Testaments. Without Jesus, as the Messiah, the whole message and purpose of the Old Testament is incomplete and unfulfilled.

The third point about biblical relevance is that descriptions of faith, both of individuals and groups, within the texts fit in remarkably well with Fowler's stages of faith development. It leaves one asking, 'Did Fowler just take it from the Bible, or did the Bible take it from Fowler?' It has been said that if all the books of the Bible were totally destroyed and lost, they would be re-written in a generation through people's experiences of life and their faith.

The final, general point I wish to make is that running through the Bible, from beginning to end, are several great themes of faith. These are the big issues of life that are always with us such as: evil, suffering, salvation or deliverance from evil, love and the nature of personal relationships, both with other human beings and with God. Underneath all these themes runs the constant struggle or battle to understand these things and make sense of them. It is the big themes that matter, not the minutiae of secondary material, or taking individual texts out of context in order to prove a point. The Bible is both big and noble in its great themes, and also brutally honest in its exposure of the dark side of human nature.

Bearing this in mind let us now turn to specific people who illustrate this in terms of faith development, and in particular universalizing faith.

11.1.1 Abraham

The story of Abraham is found in the book of Genesis, chapters 12 and 13. It is an important early story of faith, vital as a basis for understanding the Christian, Jewish and Muslim faiths. Abraham can be said to be an archetype of faith for all people, and of God's promise to him, that his descendents shall be as the sands of the seashore in number, and that he will be a blessing to the nations. Legitimately understood, his story gives him archetypal significance for all people at all times. The Koran refers to Abraham and so does Jesus Christ; both do so as models of a life of faith. St. Paul also uses Abraham as an example of faith that takes priority over the Torah. He points out that Abraham was justified before God because he acted in trust in response to God's call, and this happened at a time when the Torah or Law had not been formulated. He uses this as part of his argument that concluded, 'For, by keeping of the law shall no one be saved.' We see this argument in both Paul's Epistles to the Romans and the Galatians. This point will be developed later when we look at Paul as an example of Universalizing Faith. I mention this here in order to show how the person of Abraham is so important in understanding faith development as told in the Bible.

Now let us see those reasons that make Abraham so important as an archetype of faith, and why he can be cited as an example of Universalizing Faith. Fowler says that the main quality of people at this stage of faith is that they are drawn beyond themselves into a new participation with and grounding in God. They are people to whom God is very real, very close and with whom they have a rich intimacy.

I see in the story of Abraham that he was very much like this. The following points are adequate illustrations:

a) Abraham was in such a close relationship with God that when he heard God he acted at once. He left Ur as God had told him and just went, not asking for any guarantees or assurances. This is a basis for a life of faith that is mature because out of a close relationship with God, or with another human being for that matter, comes a trust that does not need to be 'put down in writing with guarantees'. Trust is the basis of all mature relationships because it arises out of love, which in turn gives an inner knowledge that is reliable about the nature of the other person. This is what hearing the voice of God is about. It comes out of harmonious relationship and does not need formal written or spoken words. Abraham, as do all those at the stage of universalizing faith, had this special relationship. It is a special quality that does not lead to arrogance, as some would mistakenly think, but to true humility, which leads on naturally to the next point.

b) Abraham did not control or organize situations. He allowed the process of history, in which his life was set, to take its course and as events happened he responded to them in a way that was creative, because it was not self-centered or controlling. Arrogance arises out of selfishness and immaturity and this in turn brings about the need to control and manage events for one's own ends. The self-confidence of the kind that belongs to universalizing faith comes out of a total trust that God is in ultimate control. Hence all the individual needs to do is respond positively to God's creative activity.

On several occasions Abraham demonstrated this level of faith. The first one was in the dispute with Lot over grazing land. In this he allowed Lot to choose and he took the other course himself. The second was when God tested him by asking him to sacrifice Isaac, and the third was in choosing a wife for Isaac. The outcome of all three was that Abraham came out as it were on top. The outcome was beneficial to all concerned, a very important factor when we consider those at this level of faith.

I see it having the same content, but at a less developed level, within the Beatitudes of the New Testament, another example of how Abraham is an important archetype of faith and how Jesus made reference to him both explicitly and implicitly. At the level of universalizing faith people can truly 'Let go and let God', because they have the trust and insight to stand back from situations at the appropriate time. Less mature people easily get panicked into taking action that is in the end inappropriate or even destructive. Then God is shut out.

c) The presence of the mystical in Abraham's experience is further factor of interest. Both his relationship with the angelic figures in human form who came as messengers, and his relationship with Melchizedek are mentioned in the New Testament as indications of the special awareness he had and his closeness to God. They are indicators of this advanced stage of faith. Throughout history the mystics have always had the same kind of experiences of the spiritual world, as have all the major saints.
d) Abraham had human weaknesses, but they did not seem to matter. One aspect of this can be seen to be showing us that even though people arrive at this mature state of faith, it is not something that is a continuous state. They do not live all the time at this blissful level, but have moments of slipping back. Abraham's weakness was the most common of all human weaknesses, anxiety. This is perhaps the thing that is most destructive of faith because it drives us to seek our own solutions based upon our own view of the situation in which we find ourselves, and to do so in a very worldly way. He was afraid that others would kill him to get his wife who was very attractive. So to protect his own skin he asked her to say she was his sister. In the end the plan came unstuck, and yet despite this, Abraham eventually came out of it intact. To me this is saying that when we are at this level of faith we can afford to allow our human weaknesses to surface. St. Paul makes the remark that in our weakness we are made strong. His experience of faith, which we will examine

later, has its resonance with the experience of archetypal Abraham.

Thus it would seem that in many ways universalizing faith is a matter of going back to the beginning in a more positive and secure manner. Abraham is at the beginning of biblical faith history, but his spirit permeates it right to the end and is affirmed in Jesus, whose incarnation reflects both alpha and omega, the beginning and end. In the life of an individual human being, so much of universalizing faith is a return to the early infantile bliss of the undifferentiated kind. The beginnings and ends are so closely related that they cannot but influence each other.

11.1.2 The Torah and the Prophets

In the faith history set out in the Old Testament the Torah, or 'law', and the prophets come after Abraham in chronological terms, but in faith terms they are regressive. Why should this be? I would dare to suggest that it is to do with the sinful stupidity of human nature. We human beings are so bogged down with the trivia of this world that we do not seem able to allow ourselves to trust God in a childlike way. We seem to have to learn its value through a tortuous course of painful trial and error that arises out of our own obstinacy. It is so hard for us to learn to love and be loved, and creative in all our relationships, that we tend to regress into a world of protective laws and procedures, status symbols, worldly goal-orientated achievements, CVs and certificates, in order to feel OK as a person. In purely faith terms the Children of Israel were given the Law or Torah by Moses because they could not live in the state of faith that Abraham had. This meant, in Fowler's terms, that they were being disciplined into a synthetic-conventional faith. After Abraham they had fallen from the highest level of faith, and a redemptive process was required. They had to go backwards in order to do that.

The Old Testament Prophets are the next step on in faith.

They represent the individuative-reflective stage. Their message is a critique of the priestly classes whose role it was to maintain the synthetic-conventional system which was rooted in the temple. A good example of this is Amos, who in chapter 7 of his book is seen confronting Amaziah, the priest, in a very individuative-reflective versus synthetic-conventional dialogue. The other factor in the prophets is their proclamation of the messianic hope, which is that God will send a special person who alone will be able to lead them on into a more mature and fulfilled way of faith. Isaiah and Jeremiah are the main bearers of this message. Isaiah, with his servant songs, especially Isaiah, chapter 53 and Jeremiah in chapter 31, where talk is of God's laws being written within the hearts of people so that they will act spontaneously in love towards God, and each other, and not have to be continually exhorted to keep 'the law'. The prophets point the way towards the possibility of a growth into universalizing faith and see the coming Messiah as the one through whom it will be made possible.

There is one very important book in the Old Testament which deals with the conjunctive stage of faith, and that is Job. It is in faith terms the link between the prophets and the New Testament. This has been dealt with fully in Chapter 10 on conjunctive faith. As a book it stands out on its own in the Old Testament writings.

11.1.3 The New Testament

Jesus Christ is the very essence of the New Testament. Without him it would not exist. Therefore we begin with a look at Jesus purely in terms of faith development. He would fit the bill perfectly as one whose life was lived out at the stage of universalizing faith, and his whole life and work was directed at encouraging people to live at this level of faith themselves. It is, in my opinion, one of the greatest failures of the Christian Church that it has not made much of an attempt to follow its master and founder in this respect, but has been content to remain predominantly at the synthetic-conventional stage almost throughout its history. It would even seem to have persecuted those of its members seeking to move on beyond it, because they pose a threat to the stable but restricted comfort of this stage. This is so evident in ecumenical relationships today. Here I quote Bishop Stephen Neill:

> It is, of course, true, whatever denomination you may happen to belong to, that the majority of your good churchgoers will be living under law and not grace. The human heart is incurably legalistic. We prefer the limited demands of an ecclesiastical system, heavy though they may be, to the unlimited demands of genuine surrender to Jesus Christ. (From *On The Ministry*, p.101, SCM Press)

In short, it is safer and more comfortable to stay at the synthetic-conventional level than to move on. People who do move on and aim for universalizing faith become a threat to the many who are afraid to do so. In the Gospels Jesus' greatest conflict was with the Pharisees, men who were masters at maintaining the synthetic-conventional system inherited from the Old Testament. We now look at this.

In St. Matthew's Gospel 5:29, Jesus says to his listeners: 'Unless your righteousness exceeds that of the scribes and Pharisees you cannot enter the kingdom of heaven.' In the same Gospel later on during his comments known as 'The seven woes to the Pharisees' (chapter 23), Jesus castigates the Pharisees because they hold people back from entering heaven by their religious impositions. To me this is about those well dug into the synthetic-conventional stage of faith preventing anyone from moving on beyond it, either through ignorance or possibly willful control and exercise of power in a worldly manner. How often do Christian churches do this very same thing?

However, it would be wrong to say that Jesus did not recognize the need for people to spend time being nurtured at this level. He seems to take great care to say that the law must be respected. It was a necessary thing for spiritual development, but it was a stage through which people passed, and for a full faith they need forms of nurture that take them beyond it, not a controlling discipline that holds them too tightly within it. This is what I understand Jesus to mean when he said that he came to fulfill the law and not to destroy it.

The sign that people have moved beyond 'the law', or the synthetic-conventional stage of faith, is the quality of their personal relationship with God. All those who have done so and enter the universalizing stage act, speak and think as though God is with them all the time, like a close and very trustworthy intimate friend. They do not live by rules and doctrines, but in an intimacy with God similar to that of lovers. They are totally permeated with God's presence and this is obvious to all who know them. Nothing needs to be said. Jesus was like this, and the best verbal expression of his beingness is The Lord's Prayer: 'Our Father in heaven…' Anyone who can pray this from the depth of their being is expressing this trusting intimacy with God, and must be at the universalizing stage of faith.

The Beatitudes or Sermon on the Mount, in terms of faith development, is a statement of what their life is about, for those at the universalizing stage of faith. It is not a moral code, because it is impossible for anyone to live up to it in their own strength, neither is it a theological statement. Those things rightly belong to the synthetic-conventional stage of faith. The words simply say that those who have a certain kind of faith will be like this. They will be very close to God in such a way that those things of this present age, which bother most people, won't bother them because their faith in God, the true and living God, has taken them beyond. This is why the Sermon does not make sense to most people.

It is too great a task to attempt an exposition of the whole of the Beatitudes here; but to fill out as illustrations what I have just said, I will comment on three of them.

i) *Blessed are the meek, for they shall inherit the earth.*
The average human reaction to this would be, 'Rubbish, it never works that way!' The clever, strong and aggressive who work hard and apply themselves inherit the earth. For many years I would have felt this way, and as a result avoided this statement of Jesus. Now, however, I am beginning to take it seriously and wrestling with an understanding of it. The truth I am in the process of discovering is that now I am a pensioner I have no power in this world's terms. People who have worked hard and aggressively to inherit some part of the earth are now clapped out and looking for an inner peace that they see I thankfully have. There is more to it than this, but it seems that when we can truly let go and let God, He acts to do things we can't. Although many Christians will say in theory that they believe God rules the world and the whole of history, most of the time they live as though He does not. 'The meek' are living as though God does rule, but it takes a long faith journey to get to that point.

ii) *Blessed are the pure in heart, for they shall see God.*
My pastoral experience has taught me slowly the truth of this. God can only show Himself to people who recognize and accept what they are truly like, warts and all. When we do this, our spiritual eyes become open to see God. I know this to be true from experience. It is in our nature to put on a good face, try and cover up or avoid our weaknesses, try hard to prove ourselves, and as part of this immature proving process we invent clever intellectual arguments to disprove God. We seem to be so easily deluded into thinking that we are cleverer and more able than we really are, and the worst part of this is the struggle for morality. Trying to be good in our own strength is terribly destructive, whose outcome is invariably one of setting up others

as scapegoats upon which to project our own negatives because we can't accept them within ourselves. My experience has taught me that the truest wisdom is a loving heart, because the purity of heart that opens us up giving us eyes to see is an act of God's grace. Then none of our failings and weaknesses matter. Sin does not lie within these things, but within our denial of the truth about ourselves.

iii) *Blessed are the poor in spirit, for theirs is the kingdom of heaven.*
I have always seen this as being more obvious than most of the other Beatitudes. Heaven is spiritual state. Hence, if we desire it, all that needs to be done is to recognize one's spiritual lack and God will supply it. Those who really want to enter the kingdom will soon see their lack because its state is in such contrast to worldly ways that it cannot be confused with them. The basic issue is that of desire. When the desire is there, the rest falls into place. I think that the total desire required tends only to come in the right way when one enters the universalizing stage of faith.

I conclude this look at Jesus Christ as an example of universalizing faith with the statement that there is much I have not said, and a study of the whole of Jesus' teaching is a valuable thing to do, especially His lesser known and often more difficult sayings. They all point us directly in the way of universalizing faith.

11.1.4 St. Paul

I use St. Paul here as an example of how the movement towards universalizing faith is not always a smooth one, with distinct beginnings and endings to each stage. There is much struggle, pain, and anxiety involved about one's ability to cope. At times we enter for a while into one stage, and then fall back into the previous one before returning more securely to the one we fell back from. St. Paul has always intrigued me as a person because of the inconsistency in his writings. He goes from brilliant spiritual insight, shining out with inspirational love and acceptance, (such as 1 Corinthians 13) to pedantic small-minded nit-picking, such as 1 Corinthians 11:1–16).

My interpretation of all this is that we have recorded in the book of Acts and the Epistles of Paul evidences of his growth in faith from that of a synthetic-conventional Pharisee, through the subsequent stages into that of universalizing faith. Because he is so open and honest in his writings, we look into the heart of a man struggling all the time to leave the Pharisee behind and enter into the freedom of spirit Jesus Christ wants to give to all; a spiritual freedom that, in the end, leads to universalizing faith. Together with this private struggle we see the struggle to give leadership to a very motley bunch of people, all at different stages of faith. The responses of such people are often confusing, difficult to understand, and at times threatening to one's own inner struggle and what can be seen as the good of the whole community.

I see all this going on in the life of Paul, and I also see it in my own life and many others with whom I have talked about these things. For these reasons I am so grateful to Paul, even though I may not have liked to have him as a close friend!

Let us examine the evidence of the stages of faith in the life of Paul.

i) Synthetic-Conventional.

This is well demonstrated in the book of Acts. We see him at the beginning as the enthusiastic synthetic-conventional Pharisee, vigorously promoting and defending his faith against the threat of the new Christian movement. He also confirms this in his own words, writing at a later date in the Epistle to the Galatians, chapter 1 from verse 11. It was Paul's experience on the road to Damascus that moved him out of this stage (Acts 9). It is interesting to note that most people need some deep spiritual experience, often of a shocking nature, to enable them to move on from this stage because it can become a very secure and comfortable spiritual state to be in.

ii) Individuative-Reflective.

We only have hints at this both in Acts 9:10 and Galatians 1:16–17. The strong suggestion here is that Paul needed to go away and work a few things out for himself so that he would be able to have a good intellectual framework by which he could understand his new state of faith, including the resurrection and ascension of Jesus, his divinity and Messiahship. In Acts 9:22, 28, 29, we have the suggestion that he was very argumentative, operating at a very intellectual level, so different from his later more mature preaching, and had to be rescued by the brethren. This is a mark of those at the individuative-reflective stage.

iii) Conjunctive.

The whole of the Epistle to the Romans can be understood as a work about conjunctive faith. Paul struggles to bring together the conflicting parts of himself. He begins by talking about paganism in relationship to Christ. In chapter 8 the subject is the place of the Holy Spirit in prayer and redemption, and in chapter 11 the place of the Jewish Faith in the whole scheme of things. All these bits of experience and their conflicts are being worked into an inclusive pattern of faith, a key task at the conjunctive stage. The other task at this stage is that of being able to live creatively with paradox, and is well expressed by him in 1 Corinthians, chapter 1, from verse 17. Here Paul talks about weakness being strength and the wisdom of men being foolishness to God. These two themes can be seen in other writings of Paul.

iv) Universalizing Faith.

We get glimpses of this stage mixed in with the conjunctive. The most striking example would be the whole of 1 Corinthians chapter 13, the famous discourse on faith, hope and love (see page 231). Another example is 1 Corinthians 1:17–23, and 2 Corinthians 1:3–11, where Paul shows an understanding of mystical experiences of God and ends with the paradox: 'When I am weak I am strong.' A paradox taken on at the conjunctive stage can be fully lived out at the universalizing stage. Finally in 2 Corinthians 12:1–15, we have another indication of Paul's mystical awareness that points to him living at the universalizing stage of faith.

This has been rather a 'thumbnail' sketch of the faith history of St. Paul and could well be developed further. For our present purpose it is enough to show his general movement through the faith development stages.

11.1.5 The Johannine Writings

These writings are: the Fourth Gospel, the three Epistles attributed to St. John, and the Book of Revelation. I only wish to refer to two specific texts, but before doing so comment on this group of books as a whole. Even a casual reader would note that they have a common style, language and general approach that is different from that of the rest of the New Testament. They are all written at a later date than the rest of the New Testament, and their interpretation of Jesus is of a more reflective and developed nature, which would appear to be the result of the influence of time, personal experience and the activity of the Holy Spirit. In them we get very clear glimpses of that state of universalizing faith into which Jesus was seeking to lead people during His life on earth. It seems to me that, when on earth, He began a process towards this end which matured and grew slowly after His death and resurrection. This has a continuity in Orthodox and mystical theology, especially the thought of St. Gregory Palamas which he calls 'The Deification of Man', the concept being that within the believer the risen Christ causes a slow and gradual transformation, the end of which should be a restoration of man as a reflection, indeed 'image' of God. This is a universalizing faith. We return to this later, but now I just want to refer to the two texts that point to universalizing faith in the Johannine books. This will conclude our look at the scriptures.

Firstly, the Prologue of St. John's Gospel 1:1–14. If I was asked to give one passage of scripture only to explain the essence of the Christian Faith I would give this one and suggest it be read, prayed over and meditated upon for several years so that the full meaning can be absorbed. To me it is a complete description of universalizing faith and of how to enter into it. Jesus is seen in His completeness as 'The Word' or more accurately 'The Logos' who is the true light that enlightens all men. The emphasis is on 'All' because universalizing faith is a state that is beyond all religious structures and strictures into which all are called. We have to pass through all sorts of developmental stages, religious, social and psychological. Each has their place and value, but they are not an end in themselves. If we make them so we ultimately destroy the very faith they are there to nurture. This passage sets out the message of the whole Gospel, which is that faith is something that must grow and develop beyond where we now are, and the purpose of Jesus, the Christ, is to be an agent of such growth for all mankind.

Finally, the First Epistle of John. This epistle seems to assume that a state of universalizing faith exists. Two texts are an indication of this. The first is chapter 3, verse 6: 'Anyone who lives in God does not sin.' This statement could apply only to those well into universalizing faith because these are the only people whose lives are lived so closely to God that they have grown beyond the power of sin. The second is chapter 3, verse 21: 'If we cannot be condemned by our own conscience, we need not be afraid in God's presence.' This assumes a person's closeness to God of such a nature that there is complete harmony. God's will and thoughts become the believer's will and thoughts. This again points to a state of universalizing faith. It is also a fulfillment of the Lord's Prayer in a person's life, a fact that again underlines the purpose of Jesus, which is to lead all humanity on to this level of faith.

11.2 The mystics

'Mystics' have existed throughout the whole history of the Christian Church. Some have been made 'saints' and some have not, but their writings all show strong indications of universalizing faith. It is for this reason that reference will be made to some of them. The strongest indicator lies in the fact that mystics seem to be able to have very direct contact with God, who is as real to them and as solid as the earth upon which they tread. They also had attitudes and a morality that was outside and above those prevailing in their time. They lived most of the time in a different world from their contemporaries, yet were not 'one-off oddballs'. All of them, even if their lives were separated by time, language and race, had a very common spirituality and experience of God. At one time or another many were declared heretical by the official Church councils.

I find this last point interesting because, in terms of faith development, the Councils of the Church, and most of its leaders, would be at the synthetic-conventional stage, a stage that would not understand mystical experiences and would be threatened by them. As we have already seen, conformity and control is a characteristic of the synthetic-conventional stage, but by the time even the conjunctive stage is reached, these things cease to matter.

This tension has always existed from the time of Jesus and the Pharisees in the New Testament up until the present day. I also suggest that the renewed interest today in the works of the mystics could be due to the inadequacy of church structures, being predominantly synthetic-conventional, in meeting the needs of many for nurture in their faith. This in turn could be seen as a factor in the historic development of the Christian Church. In its earlier development, and especially during the Middle Ages, it needed to express its faith in varied synthetic-conventional terms. This is a necessary and normal part of faith formation, but now these structures are not needed in the same way. I say 'same way', because for many they are still required and always will be, but for growth and development into our full faith potential, both individually and corporately, more is needed, and the mystics have something to offer in this respect. Let us now take a brief look at some of them.

The following names are quite well known, Meister Eckhart, Mechthild of Magdeburg, Julian of Norwich, Hildegard of Bingen, Teresa of Avila and St. John of the Cross. All of their writings reflect aspects of universalizing faith. All lived at a time when the Church was dominant in society and its faith was expressed in very synthetic-conventional terms, and most of them were women at a time of male dominance in the Church. I find these facts interesting because these people were, in a way, ahead of their times. Whereas they were very much a part of the prevailing system, they were at the same time reaching beyond it. The faith they had was dynamic and relational, not legalistic, restrictive or expressed in a systematic way. It showed the very strong feminine side of human nature. This balances the intellectual aridity of masculine rationalism, and is an essential part of a creative relationship. This thread of emphasis is also sexual in a very deep way, and reminds us that the most creative, healing and deep human relationships are sexual ones in the widest sense of this rather abused word.

Here I note that the New Testament uses the imagery of the bride and bridegroom to describe the relationship between Christ and the Church. Also, the Old Testament's *Song of Songs* is a book about deep loving relationships between God and his people. Indeed, the only command that Jesus gave to His followers, that He claimed underlined everything, was the command 'to love one another as He loved' us. Love is a fulfilling of the Old Testament's 'law', and this is both a mark of universalizing faith and a sign of human maturity. Fromm, in his book *The Art of Loving*, said that the ability to love and be loved without strings attached is an indicator of human maturity. So few people get this far in their practical and broadly spiritual progress because too few get to the faith stage that makes that possible, but I think the mystics did.

The following quotation from Mechthild of Magdeburg [circa 1250] illustrates this. It speaks of a deep and very intimate relationship between God and a human being. The very thing Jesus Christ spoke of in the Gospels which caused such offence to the religious leaders of His time, and has often done so ever since:

> The Godhead rings
> Humanity sings
> The Holy Spirit plucks the harp of the heavens
> So that all strings resound.
>
> When I shine, you shall glow.
> When I flow, you shall become wet.
> When I sigh, you will draw my divine heart into you.
>
> When you weep in longing for me, I will take you in my arms
> But when you love, we two become one being.
> Then we can never be parted.
> Rather, a blissful abiding
> Prevails between us.

I end this section on the mystics by making a final reference in a little greater detail to one whom I think is most relevant to our subject, Joachim of Fiore [1135 -1202]. He was opposed to the theological fashions of the day and managed to get his teaching on 'the trinity' condemned. The current fashion was that theology was a science, and the philosophy of Aristotle was its basis. Because of this basic assumption, all theology was seen as a result of rational thought only. This was viewed as an error by Joachim who stated that theology should be based upon intuitive insights which were outside the realm of rationalism. One could therefore call his approach to theological thought as being a mystical-dynamic one, whereas the prevailing approach of the time was rational and theoretical.

Although Joachim was a very likable man in his locality, in the wider theological world he was disliked and opposed. It is said that he openly showed his emotions, especially when saying the mass, and could easily be moved to tears. Even today he is greatly revered as a saint in the region of Italy in which he lived, and has a local drink, still available today, named after him! The impact he had on those close to him was obviously great, and for the good. I think this is also common with those at the universalizing stage of faith. Those close to them are aware of that extra dimension which is generally called 'Godliness'. Those who did not like him, such as Thomas Aquinas, were always people whose lives were remote from him and therefore disliked his 'reputation' as they had received it, rather than known the person himself. Perhaps it was because of their remoteness that they neither knew nor understood Joachim, and this remoteness was most probably geographic, social and relational. It was always the systematic theologians who opposed him. I see this as yet another example of the tension and misunderstanding that there is by those at the synthetic-conventional stage towards those at the universalizing stage.

In the modern world Joachim still has a following among those who understand his visionary teaching and appreciate the revolutionary and developmental nature of faith. Joachim presents theology as being dynamic and creative, not static as in the case of systematic theology and dogmatics. Cardinal Ratzinger (now the present Pope) saw him as the father of liberation theology, while Dietrich Bonhoeffer, himself one who showed the marks of universalizing faith during his imprisonment and death under the German Nazi regime, was very attracted to him.

Joachim's teaching on the nature of faith was not as developed as Fowler's, but it had the same progressive thrust. He said that a person's life of faith would develop in three stages. These stages could not be neatly divided, but would have overlapping stages in which one could not clearly distinguish which stage a person was in. There could also be times of regression.

The three Joachim stages were as follows:

i) Old Testament – The stage of God as Father
In this stage people lived under the law. Joachim also called it the age of fear because the motivation that sustained the faith was fear that if one got it wrong, then the Father would punish. I see this as being very close to Fowler's synthetic-conventional stage, and one in which many people stick today. Joachim said that in this stage people related to God as slaves.

ii) New Testament – The stage where Jesus Christ is central
This was designated as being the age of faith. Those in it were sons of God and brothers of Jesus Christ. They had ceased to be slaves of God under the law. In Christ they entered a new status. This meant they were delivered from fear, and could dialogue with, or even confront God, because Jesus had enabled the change of status from slaves to sons to take place. I equate this to both the individuative-reflective and conjunctive stages of faith.

iii) The stage of the Spirit
Joachim saw this third as the stage in which the believer's relationship to God was that of friend. It has all the nature of the mystic's intimate relationship with God as one sees it expressed in the above quotation from Mechthild. He called it the age of love in which the command of Jesus, that we should love one another as he has loved us, would be fulfilled. He also saw this as a most creative stage of faith in which the Church would

> develop spiritually, and new orders and movements would be formed by those who had reached this stage. We should see this as arriving at universalizing faith, within our time, Mother Teresa of Calcutta as an example.

Finally, I end this section by recording my own experience of universalizing faith, as observed over a period of 50 years in pastoral ministry, and 58 years on my own faith journey.

Firstly, from my pastoral experience: I would claim that I have met about a dozen people, all of them elderly, who have entered into this stage of faith. They have all been an inspiration to me, and especially the one or two with whom I have been present at or near their death. Their life was lived at a deep level of peace within themselves, they saw the best in others, and the God of Love was ever present with them. In every case I enjoyed being with them because they transmitted a sense of joy within an aura of divine awe. My involvement with them was in most cases when administering the sacrament of Holy Communion.

I suspect that Fowler found it hard to give examples of universalizing faith because he lacked the hands on, face to face, and intimate relationship with lots of people that those in pastoral care tend to have. I find it sad that this identification applies to only a dozen or so people out of thousands. The vast majority of those with whom I have come into pastoral contact have been tortured souls, made bitter and twisted by their experience of life. Yet in most cases their lives have not been as hard as the small group in whom I have found inspirational faith. I see them as those who under the pressures of the material world took wrong turnings early on and could never get back on course. Often these tortured folk had a form of religiosity without knowing God; an obsessive, compulsive, inner spirit that drove them further from God the harder they tried to be good. Just like highly moralistic humanists whom I have met, they are very sad people.

Fowler is correct in saying that few enter this stage, but then

Jesus Christ said the same. I hope to take this issue up again in the conclusion.

Secondly, from my own experience while on my faith journey, I can easily recognize within my own faith history all of Fowler's stages. I would put myself now predominantly at the conjunctive stage, but with short periods of time when I enter the universalizing stage. However, I do not stay long in this stage, but, when in it, I am aware of a new quality of life coming into me. Since passing the age of 65 I have had more time to set aside for contemplative prayer. It must have been about ten years earlier that I first became interested in contemplative prayer. But when I began practicing it I had a hard time, because I was entering the conjunctive stage and all my hang-ups and unresolved bad experiences from the past surfaced regularly. Slowly these became resolved in one way or another, and then I became deeply at peace with God and myself, but not with the world around me. I found this troubling. It threatened my inner peace whenever I had contact with it, because it was the culture in which most people lived. When I cut myself off and lived in my own little world with God and one or two people I trusted, I was always extremely happy and had a very deep inner joy. The question for me then was: 'Do I cut myself off from this horrible world that threatens me and is beginning to make me hate and despise it?' As this formed about 90 percent of what was going on around me, cutting myself off from it did not seem feasible, so I made it a point of specific prayer for quite a period of time and as I write it remains at the center of most of my prayers.

I will end by quoting a recent experience from my prayer time, recorded in my journal, which I see as being a brief entrance into the universalizing stage of faith. I say a brief stage, for I don't believe I am there yet and have a feeling that there is a long way to go. However, I am certain that it is only through prayer that anyone gets there, and as St. James says in his Epistle, we have to learn to pray in the right way as well, (St. James, 4:3).

Again I will deal with the subject of prayer and spiritual growth later. The words that came to me were:

> *There is a knowing beyond knowing when one does not need to know any more.*

These words came to me when I was meditating on the subject of faith. I asked God how we become fully aware of 'Divine Truth' in such a way that we harmonize with Him, fully trusting, to that point where, as it says in St. John's first Epistle, *Perfect love drives out fear*. So often the motivation for knowing, or collecting information is fear. When love drives out fear there are many things we do not need to know. Having divine knowledge, which is pure gift, frees us from this obsession that drives the world. This kind of freedom seems to me to be one of the main marks of universalizing faith.

I had become aware in myself that for brief moments from time to time I entered that position. As I pray contemplatively I often enter the 'Prayer of Silence' when all is God and God is all, I am in Him and He is in me. At such times the world's affairs are trivial and passing – poetically just like ripples on the surface of a lake stirred by a puff of wind. But, for a lot of the time those trivial things of the world become threatening and I struggle to overcome them. I become very angry and uptight about them. Then, eventually, after the passing of some time and much agonizing, I return to God in the mode of contemplative prayer, and the worldly troubles melt away.

When I relate this experience to my own faith history I see that this pattern has always been there in a small way. It has a very objective aspect to it in that I have seen many of the things out there in the world that threaten me perish, leaving not a trace behind. Those things that initially seem to be faith destroying become so no more; they destroy themselves, and in the end are faith affirming events.

I see this as an example of how faith develops of itself in those who engage wholeheartedly in the struggles that this present world puts before us, and do so on the basis of their own inability to cope alone, learning slowly how to pray aright, both trusting God for the outcome of the prayer and also learning how to listen into the Divine with the ear of faith. In the end all such people will be brought into the fullness of universalizing faith by the grace and love of God, but it will take time, patience, prayer and struggle. It happens because God causes it to happen within us, and we humans can only cooperate with Him by doing those things which dispose us favorably towards allowing it to happen.

The good news is that we can all get there in the end, but we have to be willing to turn away from the bad habits into which this world conditions us, so stealthily and subtly that they easily happen to us without us knowing. We need to repent in the true meaning of the word; to turn fully towards God and away from all that cuts us off from Him. Cleverness is not required, just an honest and willing heart.

> *Blessed are the pure in heart, for they shall see God.* (St. Matthew, 5:8)

11.3 Some concluding reflections on the nature of faith

I conclude this chapter with some reflections upon the relationship of faith to other important issues we have to face in life. This is a very personal exercise based totally upon my own experience. For me faith is the most important thing I have, everything else comes second, or arises out of it. I realize now that this has always been the case in everything I have done. My study of Fowler in the second half of my life has given me the means of having a deeper understanding of this which has helped me considerably, and is the single most important driver of this whole book.

Because the very nature of faith is inward, that is seated and developed within the individual's psyche, or personality, it is possible to allow it to become so introverted and cut off from the present material world in which we have to live that it can be seen as an individual's personal whim, fancy or even escape. If this is the case, then the faith held is false or at least inadequate. A full, living, and dynamic faith is so creative and powerful in its motivation of an individual that it radiates outward in ways that challenge, change, and deeply affect the affairs and nature of the present material world. A sound faith, as Irenaeus of Lyon claims, makes us 'Fully human and fully alive'.

I believe that the whole process of history would support this assertion. Two contrasting examples of this are the Methodist Revival of the 18th century, and the Communist Revolution of the 20th century. There are innumerable others, of many kinds and with differing effects, but they all originate in the faith, religious or otherwise, of certain exceptional individuals. Of course there are many other complications to consider when one examines these historical movements, but one common fact is that their origins are always in the faith of an individual, or group of individual people. The associated powers are personal and inward in origin.

Having stated the importance, and indeed, the priority of an individual's faith, I now wish to make some comment upon how this relates to those things that by their very nature belong to the external and material world. The two major ones I have in mind are morality and institutions. I choose these because they have been a major part of my wrestle with life in this world. Also from my experience in counseling and spiritual direction over a period of about forty years, these subjects are ones that a vast majority of people have problems with, next to the most basic and universal one of their sensitive childhood nurture, or lack of it, as alluded to much earlier in the text and examined further in Chapter 14.

My third reflection here is more in the nature of a statement. I consider it most appropriate to say something about the nature of my own personal faith, not only because, as I have already said, it is the most important thing in my life, but because it will enable all who read this to perceive more clearly 'where I am coming from'. This is a very important aspect of honest and sincere communication; the essence of what I am attempting to do.

Chapter 12

Faith and Morality

It seems to me to be an undeniable fact that there is a very strong relationship between faith and morality. All the evidence points towards this being quite a complex relationship; and within the associated dynamics, faith has the priority. Faith always comes first, and whatever a person's moral values might be, they arise out of that person's faith.

Morality is all about right and wrong values, and good and bad behavior that is based upon the concept a person has of right and wrong. People tend not to meekly accept an externally imposed set of rules for their conduct unless these rules correspond very strongly to what they believe within themselves to be right or wrong, good or evil. Throughout history there has been constant rebellion against various lawmakers of each age that in the end lead to revisions of the law. Laws enforced by authorities, political and secular or religious, only work and are obeyed if they have a good deal of congruence with the ordinary folk on whom they are imposed. Different societies and different times in history have very differing laws and conventions based upon what is a reflection of the inner faith values of the society out of which they came, and the needs of that society to preserve its health and to function efficiently.

I next examine in more detail aspects of this relationship I believe are important; and also as a demonstration of the point just made, namely, that faith has priority over morality.

12.1 Within the Roman Empire

In this case I want to concentrate upon one of the main influences that had a big impact upon this empire, and eventually, over the course of many years, some (such as Gibbon in his book *The Decline of the Roman Empire*) say destroyed it. The main positive outcome that the civilization of this empire had on the world was the *Pax Romana*, a state of stability and peace that lasted several hundred years, and cradled much creative activity, much of which is still evident today. In many ways this was a good thing, and many people individually benefited from it, but at a cost. The cost was slavery, violent death to those who questioned certain things, such as crucifixion; in general a state in which the few controlled the majority by sophisticated and well-organized thuggery.

The argument was one that persists until today, namely, that for business to prosper, law and order must be supreme and this must be rigorously enforced. To break the Empire's laws is wrong and must be punished. To keep those laws is good, and must be rewarded. The missing factor in this argument is the nature of the law. Is it universally just for all? I believe that all human made laws are inadequate, simply because they are made by human beings. However, they do have value if they are understood and interpreted in the light of the situations they address, and are adequate enough in bringing about some good when administered wisely.

The weakness of Roman law was exposed by the Christians because of the methods the Romans used as a basis for its enforcement. This was to declare that the Emperor was divine, and all citizens had to burn incense to him as a symbol of their loyalty, not just to the Emperor but also to the whole system of law, and, by implication, to the accepted morality that a good citizen would keep. No Christian could accept this without denying their faith, the basis of which was that Jesus Christ was divine and the Emperor was only a human being. They therefore refused to sacrifice and burn incense to the Emperor, and many were severely persecuted and killed. Their morality arose out of their faith which conflicted with the faith of the Roman authorities. So strong was this faith that they were prepared to die for it.

In the end this faith won after the year 321 when Constantine became the first Christian Emperor. He was converted by the supernatural experience of seeing a vision of a cross in the sky and hearing the words, 'In this sign conquer.' Of course, life was not perfect after this, but at least it improved. But the point I am making is that morality is an ever evolving thing, so that without some form of transcendent input based on faith, it becomes moribund, stagnates and ceases to be just.

12.2 During the Middle Ages

During this period the Catholic Church took over the role of the Roman Empire and to some degree spiritualized it. The supreme authority from whom morality was derived and by whom it was enforced was God, but it was God as interpreted by the Church through the person of the Pope. As with the Roman Empire before it, this was not totally negative in that it did allow a coherent society to develop in which people could to a large degree live reasonable lives in relationship to each other. We still have evidence of this in our culture today as expressed in works of art and literature. The morality was aimed at making people conform to a certain acceptable pattern of behavior by the threat of hell. Those who did not conform were ex-communicated and condemned by the official church to hell.

The problem with this approach was of an externally imposed morality. Whereas the majority would accept it, there were always a few who would not, and as time went by they grew in numbers and power, thus leading to the Reformation. Protestantism, as those who instigated the Reformation were called, still saw God as the supreme authority in matters of morality, but they did not see this authority as being transmitted through the then Church by the dictates of the Pope. They believed that God created the individual with a conscience, and that God could speak directly to the individual. They were aware of how the imposed morality of the Catholic Church at the time was more to do with power and raising money, than with the pastoral care and spiritual guidance of the individual. Long before the Reformation, certain individuals of a deeply spiritual nature, like the mystics, took the same line in matters of morality and as a result were often opposed by the official church.

It was then the faith of Protestants that challenged the existing moral order and created a new movement, but as later history shows Protestantism itself fell into the same sorts of error as that which came before it. An example of this is to be seen in the Geneva experiment of Calvin, who in his idealism sought to make Geneva a perfect city of God, a New Jerusalem. As was always the case, there were those whose behavior failed to come up to expectations. In response, he was forced to impose a strict rule and punish offenders. Some punishments were very harsh, including drowning in the lake. So, full circle, the conflict between a morality that comes from within the individual, which Protestantism championed and some still lived by, such as the Anabaptists, gave way to an imposed morality. Why did this happen? I believe it could be explained by the lack of a deep faith in God on behalf of many people, combined with a fear on the part of those in authority that this would lead to chaos and mass immorality, so undermining their authority and ability to manage society. In short, there was a fear of social breakdown and chaos.

Perhaps this is how the state of things in this world will always be. Few seem able enough to become saints who behave well from the God-given goodness of their hearts. Although this might well be the superior way of morality (so well summed up by St. Augustine of Hippo when he said of morality: 'Love God and then do as one pleases'), for the majority, a very firmly imposed morality set out in the form of definite rules is perceived by most leaders to be the only way. But, as we shall see as we move on, this leads to a very destructive tyranny.

My opinion is that these two aspects of morality will continue in conflict with each other forever, until the end of the world. The former is obviously the ideal, towards which we must journey in hope, but on the way it must always be challenging the latter one. It would seem that we live not in a stable, fixed world full of moral guidelines that are well accepted by all, but one in which a large element of moral understanding involves an ongoing dialogue that may break out into open conflict at any time, according to the historical circumstances prevailing. In this dialogue those who represent the imposed morality will be *The Establishment*, that is, those in power and social control at the time, whereas those who represent a morality that comes from within the individual are the visionary prophets. The morality of both comes from their faith, but it is faith in different things.

12.3 Within the modern world

I shall consider the modern world as that period from 'the enlightenment', as it was so called, of the 17th century to the present day. This period of history is one in which a pragmatic and materialistic outlook slowly became dominant due to technical advances that increased most people's personal wealth in the richer industrialized nations. Being more specific in terms of faith and morality, this means that from a basis of materialism it would be like having a faith saying: 'We believe that our way to happiness and fulfillment is totally, or at least predominantly, within the present material world. The spiritual world is no more than an epiphenomenon, like the froth on beer.' Morality that has this kind of faith basis spawns many things. The one is a rampant capitalism that sees profit, gaining wealth both personal and national, as the main objective of life. The other is a morality that is about distributing this wealth more fairly, and moreover gaining the power to do so. This second ethical approach saw the development of socialism, which in its more balanced form was democratic and had roots in those expressions of Christian faith found in nonconformity.

A number of forms of morality grew out of this historical situation. One was 'utilitarianism', whose basis could be said to be that whatever works for the common good must be right. Because this had very little objective faith content, it ended up confused because nobody could agree on what was the common good. One person's common good was another's personal bad. Marxism was a product-package of this materialistic approach. It saw capitalism as the enemy of the good, and saw that its destruction was the only way to create a just society. Since this package was totally trapped with the confines of materialism, it had no way out other than to annihilate all capitalists. This creed felt that when those were all dead, then the world would be perfect and just. The morality coming out of this faith was one of double standards. It was good to murder a capitalist but not a communist. So began an intensely divisive class warfare. A counter reaction to this, but with the same roots, was fascism, although some aspects of fascism were not as anti the spiritual as was communism. Fascism also sought to impose a similar morality, one of 'us and them', the perfect or super-race as opposed to inferior races who must be subdued or destroyed in order to create a perfect world. Both fascism and communism believed that to achieve the common good all its enemies must be destroyed, and the chosen people's lives enhanced and developed. From this imposed morality, based on a materialistic faith, came more than one holocaust. Between them, the communists and fascists became the world leaders in murdering innocent people, Joseph Stalin arguably being the champion in that regard.

Now these extreme forms of materialistic faith have largely collapsed. We are now in the 'post-modern' world which has recoiled from the idea of the powerful group imposing itself on individuals, retreating into a chaotic kind of bits and pieces faith, still materialistically based, in which everyone chooses their own particular style. It is a consumerist morality that reflects a society in which freedom to choose, value for money, and my right to do as I please without reference to any objective authority largely prevails as the dominant 'ethic'.

This current dominant ideology, now spreading worldwide against the broad traditions and preferences of almost all religious systems, is obviously a reaction against what has gone before in recent history. As such this is understandable, but just as the big world vision schemes of Marxism and fascism have failed, so will this approach. Modern consumerism as a faith, albeit a very ill-defined and near-conditioned one in the minds of those caught up in it, is by its very nature self-destructive for it consumes its own environment like a slowly and quietly growing cancer. It is a rejection of imposed morality, because it sees the failings of this approach; but in doing so it throws out almost all of collective morality. It has made itself vulnerable to a powerful force outside itself which it cannot control. In one word this is 'mammon', the love of money which is the root of all evil. Not money itself, but such a love of it, and all that it can buy, that those who worship at this shrine put themselves onto a treadmill to maintain it and survive. This so totally absorbs people that they have no time to develop the inner spiritual awareness that would lift them to a higher level of vision, from which they would be given 'eyes to see' and so gain insight into their situation.

Postmodernism is the full flowering of a long trend away from a balanced morality that sees the need for *both* an external dimension and an individual, internal dimension to morality. This is where we are now in the history of morality showing how complex human nature is. We can, it seems, have no simple understanding that is a, once for all times, given. All I would dare say for certain is that both faith and morality are dynamic, evolving, and developing throughout history. This development is remote from being in a straight line, but oscillates markedly, up and down, round and round. It sometimes reinvents the wheel, especially in those who have an inadequate sense of history, as did Karl Marx. Faith and morality are not static, but living. Our best way to seek understanding is to start from this point. We now turn to look at how a sense of morality develops in the individual person.

12.4 How morality develops

We have just noted how morality can be seen to develop in the course of history generally. Yet it is also true that moral awareness develops within the individual from that which is implanted in childhood nurture, and in a similar way to how faith develops. A number of people have traced this development through its stages. These vary from three to six stages. The three stages being subdivided in greater detail to produce six. These are all as viewed from a psychological standpoint and it is at this level that they have a connection with faith development.

The major work on such theory of moral development is that of Lawrence Kohlberg in the USA. His book *The Philosophy of Moral Development* (Harper & Rowe 1981) contains the most complete account of his work on the subject. He draws much of his basic material from child psychologist Jean Piaget, and collaborated with several other people in his work in the field of moral education.

Firstly we will examine the three major stages of development, which are: 'The Pre-conventional', The 'Conventional', and finally 'The Post-conventional'.

i) Pre-conventional

In the pre-conventional stage the individual basis of morality is totally related to nurture. The judgments of the infant and small child at this stage are very simple. Good is always that which satisfies, enabling the infant me to feel good and well nurtured. It is a case of being welcomed, loved and appreciated; of having needs understood and responded to. Bad is always that which bruises, punishes, or makes the infant me feel unworthy, unacceptable or dissatisfied. In essence, this phase is unavoidably egocentric, yet requires those who deliver nurture to be the opposite!

ii) Conventional

In the conventional stage the concept of good develops from that which is good for me as an individual, to that which is good socially. Awareness of morality is now being extended outward to others, so that behavior which upsets other people is bad, and behavior which pleases others is good. This level of morality grows out of development prompted by nurture from an egocentric need-based, yet undeveloped individual, into one with a new awareness that there are other people in the world with needs as valid as my own. Therefore this new awareness means that I have to consider others as well as myself. An individual's bad behavior is seen at this stage as being dangerous because of the social disruption it can cause.

iii) Post-conventional

The post-conventional stage is one at which individuals see morality as being more than just social convention. At this stage conforming to rules of the society in which one lives in order to keep everyone happy, and by so doing making oneself feel good, is not enough. The concern therefore is now more with personal principles based on a personal ethical system that is not necessarily defined by the laws of the society in which one lives. It therefore becomes inevitable that, at this stage of moral development, spiritual issues become very important – such as the right of individuals to be treated with respect and dignity, the right to hold contrary opinions to those generally held in society and not to be persecuted. This includes the right to belong to social sub-groups, such as faith groups, without being classified as deviant.

12.5 The subdivisions of moral development

Having looked at the three main stages of moral development we now turn our attention to a further enlargement of the picture by examining the subdivisions, each main stage being divided into two distinctive ones. Unsurprisingly, in reality edges blur between them, but for clarity it is helpful to make such distinctions.

12.5.1 The pre-conventional level

The two sub-stages at the pre-conventional level are punishment avoidance and reciprocal hedonism.

a) *Punishment avoidance*

The message given at this stage to the child by parents is simply: if you behave, you won't be punished. The child at this stage has no idea at all if its behavior is right or wrong, good or bad, it just does it. Similarly with regard to love, it learns about loving and being loved by being loved first, and then responding. In my experience of children, at this stage they have a definite personality in embryo. They are not a 'blank sheet' upon which the adult world can write whatever messages it wishes. Some children are more defiant and aggressive, others more sensitive and compliant, with many variations in-between. Thus the parent or responsible adult needs to understand the child's basic personality, and only punish accordingly. For some a tiny smack is essential, for others it is not, and could even be harmful. The most important thing of all with regards to punishment at this stage is love. Where there is love at a deep and mature level, any form of punishment will be appropriate and have good results. Deep love is also an outcome of maturity, and the most damaging thing of all as far as the early stages of moral development is concerned is for a child to have emotionally and spiritually immature parents or carers.

b) *Reciprocal hedonism*

When I think of this aspect of moral development I cannot help but think of dog training. It is indeed true that at this stage basic human nature does share much with the animal world. Whereas in the previous sub-stage the motivation is avoidance of punishment, at this sub-stage it is the joy of a reward. In short, this is a movement from negative to positive motivation, and both are essential in working towards a mature morality. They form a base from which to move on. When both become established in balance, then there is an established foundation for moving forward as an ethical being.

12.5.2 The conventional level

The next major stage, one of conventional morality, also has two subdivisions. These are 'interpersonal concordance' and 'maintenance of social order'. Unless the previous stage has been adequately learned in infancy and early childhood there is no foundation on which to build this one. Antisocial behavior in teenagers and socially disruptive behavior in schoolchildren all have their source in bad or inadequate nurture at the preschool stage, that phase of foundational development advisedly set within the context of committed families. Latent attempts to remedy severe deficiencies in early nurture are hugely problematic, and too often fail.

c) *Interpersonal concordance*

This is the basis of the development at this stage and arises directly out of the previous one. The well-nurtured child has already learned at home that it is personally beneficial to behave in such a way that will create for it a happy atmosphere in which to live. This experience is then carried into the wider world as it grows and has to spend most of its time living in an environment outside that of the nuclear family in which this was learned.

The child at this stage conforms to school, club, or even rules made in the playground between playmates so that they will be seen to be a good person in the eyes of authority. Schoolteachers have great authority at this stage of development, and thus hold much responsibility in the child's moral formation at a wider level socially than only within the family setting. The external authority of role models is internalized and made personal at this stage. From the influence of relationships with such-like authority figures, with whom a personal relationship is possible, firm moral formation takes place. To conform to what is acceptable in the eyes of authority is good; not to conform is bad. This is likely to be the stage at which the law abiding citizen is created, or not.

d) *Maintenance of social order*

This is a further development from the previous one which does not change basics, but takes them out of school and childhood into the adult world. Many people stay at this stage for the rest of their lives, holding the belief that the most important moral value is a society which is stable, with the rule of law and order paramount.

One can appreciate this ethic as being desirable, but it can stagnate, destroy creativity and become tyrannical, in that it cannot accept any form of deviant behavior no matter how innocuous that might be. In attempting to create a stability in which the individual feels secure, it does so at the cost of destroying some of its less conforming members. Politically this seems to have been a big issue throughout history, and as already pointed out, seems to be inevitable when one considers human nature in all its complexity. The conformist ethic is often too static, and does not allow for the ongoing development of the human spirit.

Just as with synthetic-conventional faith, this is a very important stage in development that has a very high appeal for many people, making them feel safe in a world that can be very threatening. It is so easy to want to stay in it, but if everyone did, tyrannical oppression would rule, as history shows. But history also shows that when the conventional morality of any period is replaced by a new one, eventually the new, apparently freed morality sets hard to become akin to an old conformist tyranny. This brings us automatically to consider post-conventional morality.

12.5.3 The post-conventional level

This is the level of development reached when a person's moral judgments are no longer based upon the laws and conventions of the time or society in which they live. Morality at this stage has a more abstract and philosophical basis, viewing the legalism of the conventional stage as being a set of rules made by human beings to suit the conditions of their specific society. It is perceived as being basically legal and does not sufficiently consider individual rights, special needs and differences. It is a stage in which people are aware of the complexity and weakness of human nature and look for moral guidance to authorities beyond that which is merely human with all the limitations of its mundane ways. This is a phase when worked through religious and philosophical principles become the basis of morality; and, as with the previous levels, it has two stages.

e) *Social contract*

This represents a slight movement on from the previous stage in that social order is still its prime aim, but with the awareness of how imposed moralities can become tyrannical for some individuals, it seeks an agreed morality that considers everyone and tries to protect their individual rights. The concept of 'The common good' is now dominant. The individual must always behave in a way that does not infringe upon the rights of others. What people do in private is seen as their affair as long as there are no spin-offs harmful to others. In public affairs the will of the majority is the norm, within which deviancy can take place provided that it is not damaging to the public good.

f) *Universal ethical principles*

This stage sees moral authority as existing totally outside individual and social needs. It states that there is an ultimate universal principle that is the basis of good behavior. This is beyond and above any law or tradition that is man-made. In philosophical terms Emanuel Kant's idea of the categorical imperative is an example of this stage of moral thought, whereas in religious terms St. Augustine of Hippo's maxim that one should love God and do as one pleases, is another. It could be said that Kant sees a good conscience as a guide to good behavior, while Augustine sees love in its fullest agapetic form as being the best guide.

Kohlberg's scheme has the virtue of spelling out in a reasonable way from a psychological point of view the fact that morality is not a fixed, given thing, but something that develops as society and human beings develop. Morality relates to the faith of an individual as well as to their state of psychological and spiritual development at any one time, and also to the social conditions and needs at any given period of history. Because of this developmental and evolutionary process, some could draw the conclusion that morality is all relative. What is good at one time and in one particular situation may not be so in another. I would say that there is truth in this, but it is not the whole truth, because patterns in the psychological developmental approach and in the historical approach imperceptibly move us towards the desire for an absolute morality. Such is painfully slow and hard to achieve, but it is nevertheless always present in the virtues and higher aspirations of mankind. This is now explored through an examination of a Christian, Bible-based morality.

12.6 A developed morality arising out of Christian faith

In order to come to an adequate understanding of this theme one needs to look at the whole of the Bible and not just take from it texts that support one's own ideas. The first point to reiterate is that the Bible is not just one book, but a library of books written by many different people over several thousands of years. The many books in it have their own distinctive approach, and the language also varies. It begins with basic Hebrew in the early books, then goes on to develop into early Aramaic, while finally the New Testament books are written in Greek. Within these differing languages are differing styles of writing varying from simple, semi-literate styles, such as St. Mark's Gospel, to very developed and sophisticated styles such as that of St. Luke, an educated gentile.

Behind the books of the Bible there are other documents on which some of the writers depend considerably. Some of these texts (e.g. The Epic of Gilgamesh), exist today in languages other than the biblical ones. In many cases other literature gives credence to the biblical texts. The scholarship that has gone into examining these texts is phenomenal, and has come from a wide variety of standpoints.

The variety of types of literature in the Bible is also wide. Some is historical, some mythological, some poetry, and some are collections of sermons or comments upon the current state of affairs, as with the Prophets. Some books incorporate wise sayings (e.g. Proverbs), while others are parables, stories aimed at making an important point about which readers need to think, as in the stories of Jonah or Ruth. It is interesting that Jesus taught mostly in parables because he saw them as being the best way to communicate deeper spiritual truths.

I write this as a prelude to my aim of looking at the Bible as a means of exploring a Christian morality because, without this wider awareness, it is so easy to fall into a narrow fundamentalism that could destroy a sound basis, and thereby lead to a false morality. Now I feel free to pursue my main purpose, which is to set in the whole context of the historical development of these remarkable and diverse texts a broadly based and valid understanding of Christian morality. This is not just the teaching of one person, set in the context of one particular time or situation in history, but a developing, living, and continuing theme arising out of human experience of life in this world as an ongoing struggle in relationship with the divine.

In looking at the whole Bible from beginning to end, several things become at once apparent as far as our aim of coming to an understanding of Christian morality is concerned. The first one is its practical nature, in which we see the very worst and best of human behavior. Everything that I have experienced in my lifetime exists in the texts of the Bible. All the virtues and vices are lived out to the full as I experience them. Only the clothing and technology have changed. The nature of human beings remains the same, and our struggles with life are basically the same. The texts of the Bible do not seem to have been written by 'once removed from reality armchair theorists', but by people struggling with life in all its complexities, from Abraham to St. Paul and from Isaiah to St. John the Divine.

The second thing one observes is that these struggles, and the morality that is being worked out as a result, are all done within the context of a living relationship with God. The problem of suffering as worked out in the book of Job is not merely abstract theory, but involves a face-to-face conflict with God, ending with Job having a new awareness of God and healing.

These two factors are the two fixed points out of which a Christian morality develops. This takes full account of the here and now existence of the human being in this present world with all of its pain, conflict, inadequacies and apparent injustices, yet the same time being aware of a transcendent spiritual being, God, who is available in this struggle, not by giving simple answers, but by being a Presence with us to aid us in our struggles.

These two fixed points come together in the Christian doctrine of 'the incarnation'. In the historical life of Jesus, Christians believe that Divinity visits Planet Earth as man, joining us in our struggles. By identification, for Christians this becomes a living daily experience, not a theory. It is the focal point of all the biblical texts and the starting point for developing a working morality.

With such a basis for our thoughts on morality we become open to a living and developing morality that takes account of all the differing situations of history, society, and individuals, within the context of these two factors. It fits well with Kohlberg's psychological scheme of development of moral awareness because both are about truth. In the early Church, especially the Cappadocian Fathers and Gregory of Nyssa, human nature is seen as being restless, on the move, developing towards a perfection that will ultimately end in God and in the Kingdom of God, but it will never be fully achieved in the present era. In Augustine of Hippo we have the same theme with, as we have already seen, love as the motivator. All of this is a long move on from the prescribed Ten Commandments. I would suggest this is so because the Ten Commandments reflect a pre-conventional stage of moral development, while these early Church fathers are at the post-conventional stage where universal principles are dominant.

Having drawn the boundaries at their widest point, I now fill in some of the details in this complicated picture by making reference to specific biblical texts.

In The Old Testament morality was based upon the Torah, or law. The basis of this law is expressed in the Ten Commandments (Deuteronomy 5:6–22). These are further developed in the Book of Leviticus. The basic moral concept was that by keeping this law people would be brought into relationship with God, and from that relationship would come a sound morality. The Torah, obviously, for the practicing Jew is more than just obeying a social moral code. It points beyond that to God, but in as much as keeping the law was important it can be see to fit well into Kohlberg's conventional stage. On the other hand, the New Testament's 'Beatitudes' (Matthew 5:1–12), appear to be the basis of morality. These are not a set of rules, but a series of statements about an individual person's state of being, a condition of the heart and soul that comes from within. From this state of being, a certain quality of morality comes forth, clearly an example of Kohlberg's post-conventional stage.

In these two biblical examples I have stated the two extremes to show how within its collection of books, during the course of history, concepts of morality developed. However, as is often the case with big subjects, there was no simple linear development. Our next examples will be concerned with filling in the details.

In the Old Testament we see an interesting tension between the prophetic and priestly elements. The function of the priestly was to maintain the establishment that was based upon the law. The prophetic element constantly criticized this, exposing its inadequacies. An example of this conflict can be seen in the book of Amos 7:10–17. The message of Amos is simply that God will judge Israel because of the unrighteousness of the priestly establishment who do not bring about any form of moral goodness. In chapter 8 Amos vividly describes them as a basket of overripe fruit about to go rotten. A number of other prophets at different times in Israel's history give the same message, but one that is in my opinion crucial as far as pinpointing the problem is Jeremiah. He sees quite clearly that imposing laws on people from without is doomed to failure as far as making them into good people is concerned. I will quote what Jeremiah says because it sums up all that the Old Testament prophets say about the problem of a morality imposed from without by law and points ahead to the New Testament: Jeremiah 31:31–34.

> See, the days are coming – it is Yahweh who speaks – when I will make a new covenant with the house of Israel (and the

House of Judah), but not a covenant like the one that I made with their ancestors on the day I took them by the hand to bring them out of the land of Egypt. They broke that covenant of mine, so I had to show them who was master. It is Yahweh who speaks. No, this is the covenant I will make with the house of Israel when those days arrive – It is Yahweh who speaks. Deep within them I will plant my Law, writing it on their hearts. Then I will be their God and they will be my people. There will be no further need for neighbor to try to teach neighbor, or brother to say to brother, 'Learn to know Yahweh.' No, they will all know me, the least no less than the greatest – it is Yahweh who speaks – since I will forgive their iniquity and never call their sin to mind.

12.7 The Council of Jerusalem

The Council of Jerusalem is recorded in Acts, chapter 15, and can be seen as the first council of the Christian Church. At issue was not just a theological dispute or concern of faith, but a moral issue that arose out of two things. The first was to do with tradition, the basis of the accepted morality of the time. The second was the faith experience of the early Christians as they interacted with the here and now of their times. In short it was the outcome of an interaction between the inner faith life of these early Christians and the manner in which the daily events of their present world touched them. Both of these two points of tension are equally important. To give up one at the expense of the other would mean that development and creativity would be destroyed. Hence the Council was both essential at the time, and a key to future understanding.

Now let me enlarge upon these two issues; firstly tradition. All the first Christian believers were Jews. In their tradition they had all been circumcised and lived their lives in obedience to the Torah. In the books of the law, behavior was spelt out in detail, covering every aspect of life (see the Book of Leviticus). The

Pharisees had added to these laws and thereby had developed a very complicated system of morality. Jesus had taught and done a number of things that were a little confusing for them. On the one hand he challenged the law and was very critical of the Pharisees' interpretation of it. That was one of the reasons why he was crucified. He seemed to align himself more with the prophetic tradition than the priestly (legal) one. He also said that he had come not to destroy the law, but to fulfill it. Jesus was himself a practicing Jew, and stated openly that his mission was to the lost sheep of the house of Israel (see Mark 7:24–30). Therefore, those early Christians could argue quite soundly that to be a Christian one must also firstly be bound to keep the whole Jewish law as tradition dictated.

Now, on the other hand, what was happening in the world around them as they preached was that more and more non-Jews who had never kept the laws and traditions of the Torah were believing in Jesus, and what is more, being really blessed by God. These 'gentiles' were growing in number as new converts from among the truly Jewish people declined, and even turning to active opposition.

One of the great persecutors, St. Paul, a hard core Pharisee, had been dramatically converted by the direct activity of God. St. Peter was also being subjected to some direct assaults on his traditional Jewish nurture just as a result of being faithful to Jesus and preaching the Gospel. Experience was turning the traditional world upside down. An example of this is Peter's experience at Joppa (that is modern Jaffa), as described in Acts 10.

In brief, this is what happened. A certain Roman centurion called Cornelius who was a 'God Fearer' (a term used to describe a person who was not a Jew, but who prayed to God and showed respect for Jews), happened to be saying his prayers when he had a vision in which an angel told him to send for St. Peter. He did so, and Peter agreed to come but obviously had misgivings about the rightness of getting involved with pagans. On the way Peter was praying, and he also had a vision. This vision was one of all kinds of animals used as food by pagans, but forbidden by the law to Jews, being lowered out of heaven and a voice saying, 'Take and eat.' Peter happened to be very hungry at the time, but in obedience to the law and his long established principles, he refused and even protested. When the voice persisted, the more he prayed and protested, but in the end he gave in, and concluded that God had showed him that the food laws under the new Christian order of things were no longer valid.

There was, however, more to this than food laws. Peter went to the house of Cornelius where all his servants and friends were gathered, and preached to them the Gospel of Jesus Christ. They all responded positively and were baptized into the Holy Spirit. Now these were all pagans who had never been circumcised, baptized or kept the Jewish law. God was evidently acting outside the restrictions of the old law and traditions in which Peter had been nurtured and which, to that date, had been followed by all the early Christians. From this point tensions began to build within the growing Christian community about the nature of their morality. If God could so bless these pagans outside the old traditions, and they were all growing in number day by day, what was going on?

This was the situation out of which the Council of Jerusalem came about. It was a situation in which a development of faith was taking place that was so transforming and dynamic that it challenged existing laws and customs, but at the same time having very definite roots in the traditions it challenged.

The whole of Acts 15 deals with the council of Jerusalem. It shows how the conflict was mainly between those who had been Pharisees before their conversion, and those who had not. All the evidence forming the basis of the Council's decision came from those engaged at the grass roots of the Church and who were in touch with the reality of the day-to-day lives of all its ordinary members. James who was the chairman of the council, in his summing up, made the following statement (verses 19 and 20):

> I rule then, that instead of making things more difficult for pagans who turn to God, we send them a letter telling them merely to abstain from anything polluted by idols, from fornication, from meat of strangled animals and from blood.

The whole council agreed to this and the letter was sent out. This illustrates how morality develops and changes through experience and interaction with the world in which people live at any one time. We need to note, however, that the change also comes about from the basis of a strong tradition that gives a solid background to a creative dialogue. This Council did not just happen out of nowhere. There was both a strong history leading up to it and also very present issues confronting it. Our next task is to look at this before coming to some general conclusions.

12.8 The historical fact of Jesus

It was the incarnation of Jesus in history that changed the biblical understanding of morality. In Jesus were both the strong Old Testament traditions and the contemporary events that challenged it. Let us take a look at Jesus and his teachings so that we can see more clearly how these things happened.

A key factor was the crucifixion of Jesus which was motivated by the fact that the religious leaders of the day saw him as a threat to their status as controllers of morality. In his teaching and the acts he performed he openly opposed them, and yet while doing this he also claimed that he was not opposed to the law, saying that he did not come to destroy it but to fulfill it. He was bringing about a new way of seeing things that grew out of the traditions of the time and took them to a new level of understanding. A good example to illustrate this point is the command to his disciples that they should love one another as he had loved them. This also included loving their enemies, so not following the old retribution code of 'an eye for an eye'.

In the fifth chapter of St. Matthew's Gospel we see the fulcrum on which this change in the basis of morality turns. It is the Beatitudes. From a basis of legality, that is rules that are applied by a legal system that have to be imposed, to one based upon a set of principles that grow out of an inner sense of morality that is nurtured by love and faith. The prophecy in Jeremiah 31, to which I have already made reference, is here fulfilled. The sacrificial love of Jesus by the grace of God is written in people's hearts. It is a spiritually dynamic affair, whose basis is faith in Jesus, together with an open heart that will allow the Holy Spirit to work within it.

Jesus made this clear when he said that 'unless the state of righteousness of a person goes beyond that of the scribes and Pharisees, they cannot enter the kingdom of heaven.' Legalistically imposed morality can only restrain evil at the best, but at its worst makes people evil. Jesus gives this a full expression in St. Matthew's Gospel, chapter 23, generally known as the seven woes to the Pharisees.

This stance of Jesus prompts more attention to his moral teaching consequent from the early Christians' experience of the Holy Spirit at Pentecost, the deliberations of the Council of Jerusalem being one example. The other important one is in the Gospel according to St. John. This the last Gospel to be written, and a development of the other three in that it was compiled in the light of influence from the Holy Spirit within the praying Christian community. I will refer only to chapter 16 of this Gospel because it focuses the important principle of Christian morality. Two points are made. One is that the Holy Spirit will bring to mind all that Jesus taught, and the other is that because there were many things they would need to know which they were not ready to hear when Jesus was among them, the Holy Spirit would show them these things and lead them into all truth.

Enough reference has now been made to Scripture to

illustrate that morality, as seen by Jesus, is not a static, legally imposed affair; nor are its details fixed once and for all in history. Indeed this morality grows and develops as history progresses. But neither is it something that human beings make up as they go along, or to do with philosophical systems and ideas that are purely intellectual. Its only fixed basis is love, the love of God as experienced by those who tune into it by faith; those who as the Beatitudes say know their need of God and have a pure heart. Like Jesus, I sense that the experts in morality are those who have achieved some degree of true sainthood, not philosophers and definitely not lawyers!

12.9 Concluding remarks about morality and faith

The three important points about morality that arise out of this study are:

i) There is one very difficult and practical issue in the fact that a sense of morality in people is both cultural and developmental, and not all people and cultures are at the same point of development, different levels of morality needing to be applied. In undeveloped situations, as with for example children and young people, basic morality needs to be imposed and firm boundaries given. However, as they develop, they need to be nurtured into a state of being that enables them to have an inner awareness of right and wrong, hence enabled to become mature and responsible within themselves.

This process of nurture must have a very strong faith basis for worthwhile things to ensue. Reflective self-awareness and disciplines of prayer are basic necessities. Guidance is given in the Epistle of James:

> Where do these wars and battles between yourselves first

start? Isn't it precisely in the desires fighting within your own selves? You want something and you haven't got it; so you are prepared to kill. You have an ambition that you cannot satisfy; so you fight to get your own way by force. Why you don't have what you want is because you don't pray for it; when you do pray and don't get it, it is because you have not prayed properly; you have prayed for something to indulge your own desires. [Epistle of James 4:1–3]

For a sound sense of morality, good nurture, spiritually and emotionally is essential, and this requires the context of a culture that has sound spiritually-informed values. Oh how we need more saints in charge of our education and as leaders in our society! Here Robert Burns' poetic Scots lines apply well:

Epitaph on a Schoolmaster

Here lie Willie Michie's banes;
O Satan when ye tak him,
Gie him the schoolin' of your weans,
For clever diels he'll mak them!

ii) Institutions are very vulnerable in matters of morality. This lies in the fact that within any institution, and especially religious bodies, there is a deep fear of losing control. There always were, and always will be, people in various states of moral development, a few of which will be very wicked. The fear of these people getting out of hand always forces those responsible for governing institutions to behave like Pharisees, prescribing some legalistic moral code followed by methods of enforcement which damage. I believe it was ever so and always will be. Therefore the best we can hope for are a few saints in key positions of authority who know how to flex and bend prescriptive rules in an appropriate way.

Jesus told a parable to try and enlighten us in this respect, in St. Luke's Gospel 16:1–8. He understands our ongoing predicament of having to live in this present world and close to the kingdom of heaven simultaneously. The love of God He expresses is always ready to give us a way out beyond that which is possible in our own strength. I often ponder upon this parable myself.

iii) Finally, I believe that the roots of morality and all I have said run like a golden thread through the Old and New Testaments, and through the whole of history. All that is needed is the grace and humility to perceive that reality. The basis of a sound morality is evident. It lies within a sound practical, emotional and spiritual nurture that comes through the faith of those who above all desire goodness, truth and beauty, indeed 'sainthood' in the potent sense of the word.

Chapter 13

Faith and Institutions

Institutions are necessary elements of human society. People create them because they need them, and when they are created they seem to take on a life of their own, and people are affected by them in various ways. They can be a basis for stable government, a means for carrying out good works such as a hospital or educational institution, or as means of economic production that runs factories which produce goods and create wealth. Churches also have an institution whose aim it is to form structures that can give people a formation in faith as well as ones for worshipping God. The history of mankind shows these things very clearly. It is impossible for people to live in a society without the creation of institutions. Indeed it is these institutions that are essential for what is known as civilization.

There is however a downside to this generally positive and essential nature of institutions. This is simply that because they are human creations they contain the failings of human nature. Hence, over a period of time institutions can become corrupt and thereby cease to fulfill their originally intended functions.

In adulthood I recall some of the wise things my father used to say. At the time I did not fully appreciate these, but now, many years later, I have come to see their wisdom. One, often repeated, was:

> Beware of all institutions, including the Church. They are all human creations and have within them elements of corruption. You must be able to discern those elements of corruption and find ways round them.

This considered wisdom points out two important things about institutions in a very balanced way, one positive and one negative.

The positive matter is an awareness that institutions are essential. Without them civilized society is impossible, and this in turn means that our human well-being on a day-to-day practical level would be impossible without institutions that work at an adequate level. Perfection is impossible in this present world, but adequacy is essential. The negative side is that institutions have within them areas of corruption that can scarcely be avoided. When the degree of corruption becomes too great and the institution ceases to function, then reform or even abolition of a particular institution is necessary, but this happens only in extreme cases.

History demonstrates that in cases where revolutionaries totally destroy old, well-established institutions, what follows is often even worse and less stable. Two examples of this are the immediate aftermath of the French Revolution and the Bolshevik Revolution in Russia.

My father's comment on the nature of institutions is wise because it is balanced, for it recognizes two abiding truths: first that we need institutions and must be very careful to respect this; and second the inevitably of their containing elements of corruption due to the frailty of human nature in creating and managing them. Having set out in these basic terms the nature of institutions, I now explore it in greater detail with special reference to faith and its nurture.

13.1 Becoming trapped and then disillusioned by materialism

We are living at a time in Britain when it is fashionable to attack our institutions, to be distrustful and cynical about them and criticizing them at every opportunity. This has I believe two sources. One could be called the ordinary citizen who seems to be very disenchanted with them all, government, church, police, National Health Service, education and so on. In fact just about everything. There would seem to be a big gap between the ordinary person who in our present culture would be called 'the consumer', and those in positions of responsibility within the institutions, generally known as 'the provider'. My contention is that many unthinking people have been trapped by the consumerist philosophy that has been thrust upon us all during the last decades of the last century. I say 'thrust' because that is how I perceive a philosophy which I dislike and consider to be evil. However, I have a very strong suspicion that most of the population, driven by the human failings of greed and selfishness, colluded with this in a way that is now causing them to be trapped by it. Trapped people, having allowed themselves to be seduced by what now seems to be powers beyond individual control, but had origins in little unrecognized things which at the time seemed harmless, now lash out in anger against those people and institutions which they see as providers that don't provide as they would wish.

In a consumerist society the theory is that the ordinary person, the consumer, has a right to demand that they are provided with what they want when they want it, no matter how unreasonable or impossible this might be. It is obvious that when the provider cannot provide in the way that is expected, conflict breaks out that is ultimately destructive, in the first place of the institution, and then of those for whom the institution should be a servant. We see this tension finding expression in target setting, performance charts, tests of all kinds, a continual round of surveys to provide statistics that are largely meaningless and misleading, plus a number of other allied bureaucratic activities aimed at boosting a failing system that is failing because its basic philosophy and interpersonal psychology is at fault.

The other source of this disillusionment is the press and other mass media. Neither tend to report events as accurately as possible with the highest degree of responsibility they can manage, but distort and manipulate topics so that they appeal to the prejudices of their readers and viewers. In a consumerist society what matters are sales and viewing figures, rather than truth and integrity. Therefore what the mass media largely reflect is not a true picture at all, but one that tends to emphasize the worst elements of our society, and, furthermore, reinforces them as being true in the minds of the disillusioned.

In this scenario, which I do not claim to be the whole truth, but a very powerful force indicating a strong degree of social sickness, we can see an age old problem. That of the tendency towards self-destructiveness inherent in human nature, one aspect of what still can be baldly called 'sin'. This is a dynamic that undermines institutions. It arises out of too much power being put into the hands of those who are either irresponsible or do not have the ability and maturity to cope with it. I call this 'bottom up' corruption because it undermines respect for those who have to run the institutions by putting them under threat from unreasonable demands, causing them to have to resort to an excessive degree of legalism simply for their own protection.

The result is that some institutions collapse because they cannot recruit the right kinds of people to run them. They also have to spend considerable time and effort following procedures of a legal nature for this self protection. One outcome of this is that it is sometimes extremely difficult to recruit head teachers. Another result is the increasing violence and abuse against doctors and nurses, and the amount of money and effort the NHS has to spend on legal action and compensation. There are more illustrations I could give, but I now want to move on to look at some more positive things in our present institutions; enough has been said of downsides.

13.2 Some observations

My experience has been that within our institutions there is a group of people who faithfully struggle on with the job they do, and give a very good service. They are always people who put the offering of their skills in service to others as the most important aspect of their work. I call them 'the vocational class', because primarily their belief is that they have gifts that have been honed to form a set of skills that is of value to the community, and to individuals within it. Their fulfillment is in doing this, and they view the institution as a vehicle that enables them to carry out service efficiently. However, this view is at odds with a consumerist philosophy where individual vocation has no place in systems that have been so rationalized as to become subservient to the profit motive. Institutions then are forced into a false value system that renders service close to being a dirty word, and elevates image, materially measurable performance, and control over its essential staff, those who do the work, as priority values. The vocationally-oriented, who give good service, are thereby slowly ground down, and can be destroyed by the dynamics of institutions that should support and encourage their personal expressions of value.

At this point we come to the other end of the nature of institutions, what I would call the 'top down' aspect, because in a consumerist based institution this is the area that thrives and gives the greatest opportunity for corruption. This is because those people who deeply need positions within an institution to give them social and economic status and a sense of well-being, through hidden insecurities and neurotic tendencies within themselves, will be the ones able to work the system for their own ends and get into dominant managerial positions. Their motivation is then most likely to be to strengthen the hierarchical structures of the institution at the expense of those on the front line of providing the service for which the institution was originally created. Strengthening the structures of the institution ultimately means more tight control over those doing the work, which I have called 'the vocational classes'. We therefore end up with a situation in which this vital group of people become crushed and demoralized between two forces: the consumers, aided and encouraged by the media, on the one hand, and that of an unimaginative and controlling management that is afraid of losing its status and being attacked by the media. In all conflicts between the media and the institution, it is the vocational classes that are sacrificed.

I am not setting up a scenario in which all management and the media is viewed as bad, and all the vocational classes good. I have no doubt at all that there are very competent managers who would see their task as vocational; likewise some within the media. What I am seeking to demonstrate is that *all institutions have a vulnerability to social and psychological pressures that have their roots in weaknesses inherent in human nature.* Of this we must always be aware. What I think is important is the philosophy that lies behind institutions and how they operate. If this is not clear and understood by all, then the balance that is needed for an institution to be adequate is easily lost. All its members must know what their role is, why they are present, what the institution's purpose is, and above all have an agreed understanding (to which all members subscribe) of its philosophy. This cannot be imposed from without but must grow organically from within the institution itself. Those who contribute most to such processes will always be the vocational classes in any well-functioning institution. When this ceases to be the case, then the health of the institution becomes in serious trouble.

13.3 Church and religious institutions

What I have just said is an observation of how institutions work, or fail to work, as observed in today's culture; a reflection on an observation, but an observation that hugely applies to this present world. I now take these observations and relate them to the churches, those institutions whose core purpose is to nurture faith.

When one considers the institutions of the Churches in Britain in the present day, any thoughtful person with a degree of spiritual understanding and experience will become aware of a dichotomy. On the one hand there is seen to be largely declining institutions out of touch with society, doing and saying things that seem irrelevant to modern life, but on the other hand there is evidence of a growing interest in things spiritual. In my own experience, since I was ordained in 1959 everything I have experienced bears this out. I give one example, that when in 1959 the midnight mass at Christmas was crowded, and the problem was one of controlling drunken people. In 2006 there were far fewer people at a similar service, but they were all faith-serious, devout and committed. In addition to this fact, I now find myself doing very serious studies, having very deep discussions with, and giving spiritual direction to more people who really want it than I did in my early days of ordination. I do not think this is just because I now have more experience. It is also because more people take their faith seriously and are more committed. Many of these things that I do now would not have had much demand in the earlier days of my ministry.

This interest in spirituality is also reflected in the increased number of people studying theology at universities and colleges. Underpinning this is the work of the Alistair Hardy Foundation on spiritual experiences, in particular that of Dr. David Hay. Recent research has shown that 67% of the population claim to have had some form of spiritual experience, and this is backed up by the latest census in which 76% of the population claimed to be Christian (reported in Hay's 2007 book *Something There*).

This obvious dichotomy points us towards a situation in which the institutions of the churches are out of touch with the spiritual life and day-to-day living faith of most of UK's citizens. We live in an age when formally joining organizations is not in vogue. One Methodist minister a few years ago said that at least one third of his regular congregation would not join and become official members. This meant that the official membership of the Methodist Church (information that the media would quote,) was in fact much lower than the numbers attending church. The ways in which statistics are taken and quoted scarcely reflect the reality on the ground in terms of how many people have a faith that is important to them. Another factor in this is an over-busy 24-7, even for some, 24-7-52 culture. People who are spiritually mature in their Christian faith cannot come to church regularly every Sunday, as used to be the case fifty years ago, because of work and other social pressures. This means that many churches often have only a third or less of their committed congregation at most services at any one time. In most cases these people are more committed than 50 years ago when congregations were much bigger.

I will say no more along these lines other than to conclude that the activities of institutional churches are not coterminous with the faith and spiritual life of the people. We live at a time when there is a mistrust and rejection of the institutions by people who do have faith and consider themselves to be Christian. This is also being experienced by other institutions, in particular political parties. The committed but non-joining are much more numerous than statistics tend to show. Outsiders, especially those in the mass media, are conditioned by their environment in a secular, consumerist society and fail to perceive the greater realities of this situation. This in turn leads to the perpetuation of half-truths, false ideas and misconceptions that have become the orthodoxy of a certain class of people who have their prejudices confirmed by it, and this gives them a satisfying comfort zone in which to live. Our present situation with regard to the state of the Church's institutions in relationship to its faith and spiritual life is very complex and in a state of change and fluidity. Our next task is to examine this situation.

13.4 Polarities in defining 'church'

A good starting point is to try and give some definition of the word 'church'. From both the Hebrew and Greek words as used in the Bible it simply means those who have been called out from the world, all who have heard God's call and responded to it. Therefore it could be said that the Church is essentially a spiritual body of people brought together by a purely spiritual process and united in a spiritual bond. The idea put forward by St. Paul that all believers in Jesus Christ are joined together by spiritual bonds to form a spiritual body called 'the Body of Christ', is expressed in great detail in several of his epistles, notably 1 Corinthians, chapter 12. The sacrament of Holy Communion is seen as being an act that re-enforces this fact in the individual, expressing and enabling faith, thereby continually reaffirming that all true believers are joined together spiritually in one unit, in essence a spiritual one. Although St. Paul first stated this in a clear form, everything that Jesus said and did affirms this principle of an extended spiritual family.

However, the whole story is not complete by simply stating that the Church is a spiritual body, because as a body of people it has to live in this present world and relate to it. An institution that has the nature of any other worldly institution automatically develops. The Church then has two aspects to it, the spiritual and the worldly, both impinging on each other. This is recognized in Christian theology within the Doctrine of the Incarnation which has its basic expression in the first chapter of St. John's Gospel with the words: 'The Word became flesh and lived amongst us.' In the person of Jesus himself, both the spiritual and material exist together, and therefore His body, the Church, reflects this fact. This, I think, is the big problem that has been with the Christian Church from the beginning and will stay with it until the end of this present era. The question I now examine is, 'How do we live with this unchangeable situation in a way that nurtures a living faith among members, and what are the main problems involved?'

The whole history of the Church demonstrates that living with the fact of its twofold nature has proved too much for human beings to be able to arrive at an agreed solution at any time. It has been a history of division that has led to much very unchristian behavior. In looking at the causes of this, it is possible to pick out one constant theme that has two extreme poles, thereby creating a very complicated situation. On the one hand there are those who see the actual worldly institution as being inherently divine, and thereby giving it more value than it actually has. This divinization of the institution is expressed in theologies at the 'catholic' end of the argument. On the other hand we get extreme protestant theologies which see the institution as not divine at all but subservient to the spiritual, a position that tends to end in fragmented individualism. There are of course various theologies in the middle that try to reconcile the two extremes, or at least balance them. When one tries to take an overall view of this relationship between the spiritual and the 'this worldly' nature of church institutions, I tend to think it is unsolvable. Hence the only way is to accept the tensions and find ways of living with those that are creative in terms of authentic faith journey. This is no easy tightrope walk. Yet we have no choice but to walk it, by the grace of God, in the best way that we find possible.

13.5 Walking tightropes of principle and compromise

Next I make some practical suggestions as to how we walk this kind of tightrope, which of course applies in varied ways within all religious faiths. I do so simply upon the basis that I have done it myself for at least forty years. In old age by grace I sustain a living faith, with a balanced optimism that supports my still active ministry within the institutional church.

This is a subject which has occupied my thoughts and prayers ever since I was ordained in 1959, when I had the biggest shock of my life as I began to experience the institutional church from inside. This experience was far worse than the one I had as a National Serviceman when I first joined the Army. Whereas my actual experience of the Army was similar to my expectations, my experience of the Church was not. I held a very idealistic view of the Church, and therefore found it hard to accept its faults. The long process of coming to terms with this had its roots in the words of my father, being that every institution has its faults and we have to recognize and accept them as a starting point from which we can then find ways of getting round them. Through struggle, thought, and much prayer I have done this.

I must emphasize that every individual must find their own way. This is no case of saying, 'do this or that and you will be alright.' It is a case of absorbing the principles or equipment that will enable a person to make their own way. Since we are all very different in our psychological make up, merely to say, 'This is how I have coped with the challenge,' is of limited help. *Each one of us has our own pilgrimage to undertake* and ultimately only the Holy Spirit can guide us. A reading and meditation upon chapter 16:1–15 of St. John's Gospel can help in this task.

A second point of importance is one of acceptance. This does not mean that we must never seek to change things. It does mean that always, in the first instance, we must accept them as they are and seek to understand them. Only when we have a good understanding of the various tensions, and of our reaction to them, dare we consider taking action. If action is needed, then in good time we will be shown what best to do. Events that are not set in motion by us will happen to set up a situation in which we can act. Rushing in to put right things we think are wrong is always dangerous, because it often creates a destructive form of resistance, and open hostility, which only serve to reinforce the situation that needs to change. These kinds of negative states of affairs are deeply fixed within the nature of institutions, including churches and the organizational apparatus of all religious institutions.

Writing in the 12th century, Mechthild of Magdeburg gives this within her spiritual text *The Flowing Light of the Godhead*:

> I have had to drain many a chalice of gall because, alas, the devil still has many a one among religious people willing to pour it out. They are so full of poison that they cannot drink it all up themselves, but must pour it out maliciously for God's children.

This is the experience of a nun living in community. It speaks of the ongoing wrestles involved between the spiritual nature of the churches and their being also earthly institutions.

13.6 Developing and practicing a spiritual life

However, living with negative situations can also be something that strengthens us. As the spiritual nature of the Church impinges upon its worldly institutional nature, there is the potential either to strengthen or to destroy individual spirits. Accepting this reality is our starting point; we must also learn of the discernment that enables us to experience the spiritual nature of the Church, its inherently true nature, and the wider realities of the cultural times. The spiritual is eternal and abiding, the house built upon the rock, but the institutional is transient so ever changing within the processes of history.

Let us now consider the under-girding nature of personal discernment. In brief, this is the due care and attention given to the nurture of our spiritual life. Time and effort must be given to reflective prayer and the growth of a spirituality that suits our personality. All valid spiritual disciplines give priority to learning to be stilled, so listening and paying attention to the Spirit of God speaking within us. Deeply authentic prayer is not easy, and Christian prayer has its own distinctive styles and discipline. This is why the disciples asked Jesus to teach them how to pray. In response they were given the Lord's Prayer as a model, and so this prayer model is a fine starting point. Here I only set out cardinal principles, rather than go into details of the variety of spiritual disciplines that respected spiritual directors can assist with.

In outline, the Lord's Prayer divides into two distinct parts. The first is about listening and tuning in to the mind of God, so aligning our wills and settling our emotions. This needs much practice, even struggle, but if we are to pray aright, it must be done. The second part is one of intercession, not for things we would like, so petition for, but those things we need.

These core needs are in brief, enough food and shelter to sustain ourselves physically, the ability to know ourselves and those with whom we live and work so that by forgiving and being forgiven our relationships with them can be creative and harmonious. We are not in this world to fulfill our own selfish ambitions, but to serve and be served in the community of the Gospel. By so doing we grow spiritually.

The final line of the Lord's Prayer, before the doxology, asks that we should be delivered from the power of the evil. We are not to be exempt from trials and temptations, but we pray to be given strength to overcome and to grow, rather than be exposed to more than we can cope with at any one time. This basic equipment enabling us to cope and overcome contains within it the gift of discernment. Evil is so subtle that without spiritual help we will easily be caught out.

This then is the only basis for real prayer, present in all the scriptures and thus other guidance only serves to elaborate upon these core elements. Now let us look at a few that I have found very helpful over the years.

I will begin with the New Testament because in the Epistles we get interpretation of what Jesus did and said, based upon the experience of those who wrote them as they sought to live out the life that Jesus set in motion at the outset. We who are Christians today are a continuation of that lifestyle.

The first illustration is in the Epistle of James 4:1–3. Here James looks at why prayers do not seem to be answered, and the outcome of this, in very practical human terms. His conclusion is that people do not pray in the right way. Their prayers are just a shopping list of selfish demands.

The second text is Romans 8, this whole chapter being worthy of much consideration, rewarding time spent meditating upon it. The focal point is verses 26 and 27. They point out the fact that much of praying is experiencing the Holy Spirit praying for us. Being totally still and silent allows us to enter into realms of spiritual reality unknown to those still trapped in a 'to do list' mentality. It allows God to drop into our minds things to pray about which start spiritual ripples within our souls, like pebbles dropped in a pond. Such ripples begin in a small confined way, and then spread out, expanding our experience slowly and purposefully over time.

The third text is Ephesians 6:10–20, a passage pointing out that we do not just contend with problems of a purely human and this worldly nature. Behind it all are spiritual forces that we cannot totally understand or confront in our own strength or by our own cleverness. It is the practical outworking of the clause 'deliver us from the evil', in the Lord's Prayer. In this prayer the word usually translated with one word, evil, is in fact, *'evil one'*. The nature of evil is personal and not an abstract idea, so well illustrated in *The Screwtape Letters* by C.S. Lewis.

I conclude this look at scriptures that enlarge upon the Lord's Prayer by making reference to two Psalms. The importance of the Psalms is not one of interpretation of the Lord's Prayer, because it was not known when they were written, but because the Psalms are universal reflections of man's struggle in relation to God and the nature of this world in which we all now live. Basic human nature is the same as it always was, and therefore all our deepest problems have changed little. An illustration of this point is in Amos 7:7–17. Here Amos the prophet confronts Amaziah the priest about the sad state of the institution of the temple and religious practice of Israel. This situation has always existed because all institutions are doomed to failure and weakness, no matter how useful and well intentioned they might have been. In the faith history of Israel we can clearly see that there was a tension between the prophets, whose function was of a deeply spiritual nature concerned with keeping 'the faith' pure and alive, and the priests whose main concern was with keeping the institution functioning organizationally. As a result there was a tendency for the priests to be limited, locked into maintaining the institution at the cost of their spiritual creativity. In contrast, the prophetic tradition was to stand on the edge of the institution and not just challenge, but stimulate spiritual development from within, so that its faith could be constantly be renewed.

The first Psalm referred to is number 65, especially verse 2. The second half of this verse is a heartfelt plea to God, 'Set me upon the rock that is higher than I.' I understand this from my own experience of feeling bogged down with all the conflicts, pressures, tensions and petty-mindedness often experienced when working within the confines of the present world and its institutions. It recognizes the need for a vision and understanding outside and above these confines that restrict and frustrate our creativity. Our release from this frustration comes only from a dynamic spiritual life that is well maintained and nurtured. It takes us into a position that is detached enough to see what is really happening, thereby helping us to discern what should be done about it. I have found the spiritual exercises of Ignatius Loyola particularly helpful here. He says that on the subject of discernment, the key issue is one of the ability to reflectively detach ourselves totally from the situation in which we live and work. This needs to be done by regular discipline so that due time is given to praying through all those issues that are disturbing us. We also sometimes need a person of spiritual maturity who is outside the institution, but has had enough experience of being within its confines, to stand upon 'the rock' with us and survey the scene below so that we can return to it with a renewed vision.

Next I instance Psalm 73, all of it very relevant because it describes all the problems experienced by those who live a life of faith within this present world. I confess that it is my favorite Psalm and one to which I regularly turn, its key verses being 16 and 17. Whereas the Psalm goes on at length about all the problems in the world, including loss of faith, these two verses state that all these things are impossible to understand by the use of human intellect alone; only by entering the sanctuary of God are we enabled to do so. So many people are blown away by this world's pressures and problems simply because they do not, will not, or cannot, enter this sanctuary regularly. Maybe they have never been shown how to do so.

Referring back to the words of Jesus in St. John's Gospel 16:23…

I have told you all this so that you may find peace in me. In the world you will have trouble, but be brave, for I have conquered the world...

… to which I add, 'and so shall we, if we enter the sanctuary of our souls, regularly seeking God's grace and discernment'.

13.7 A summing up

The institutions of all churches are and always will be infiltrated by the values of the society in which they are set, as well as being conditioned by the state of the process of history at the time. I believe that here are three broad factors of which we must be aware in these days if we are to keep our true vision and vocation, and they are: consumerism, philosophical reductionism and globalization.

Consumerism. The present Archbishop of York has well phrased our excessive retail orientation in the words 'Tesco ergo sum.' Consumerism is fundamentally driven by making money and exploiting the world and other people in order to do so. One outcome of this culture is the distortion and at times near destruction of truth. All of us can easily get caught up in pervasive consumerist drives, many to the point of shaping public images that belie or even obliterate our inner person.

Reductionism. This is a philosophical approach to life that has the basic view that everything can be understood by the human intellect alone. This can even be seen in some kinds of theology that deny mystery and try to explain everything in rational terms. This philosophy effectively spawns performance charts and a multitude of allied systems that desensitize people. The problem with reductionism is that it shuts those who implicitly hold faith in it into the smallness of their own minds. As a result they lose that 'pureness of heart' that enables them to commune with the Divine. Such philosophical currents, coming in vogue in the 1950's, found expression in 'logical positivism' whose cultural outcrop now is that we know more and more about less and less, leading us towards knowing everything about nothing that is fundamentally important. It takes time for academic philosophical ideas to work their way into practical politics, but it seems as though we live in a time when they have.

Globalization is now happening with phenomenal speed from an evolutionary perspective, and now extensively conditions our human outlook, not least spiritually. Britain and other European countries that were home to so much Christian history now have declining influences within our global world. Arguably the USA, whose founders were largely of European Christian stock, has peaked concerning its global authority, not least ethically. Managing such decline is an important priority. Yet while the institutions of the churches are part of this decline, the spiritual nature of the Church is not, and the words of Jesus still ring around sacred spaces globally. Recognition and consideration of global spiritual perspectives now looms as a central set of tasks.

Philip Jenkins' recent book *The Next Christendom* is commended in this connection, being a work of balanced judgment; indeed a careful study of how our world is today, according totally with the prophecies of Jesus as recorded in the Gospels of Matthew, Mark and Luke.

Before reviewing personal history and relational contexts for the nurture of each soul-spirit, I conclude this chapter with Shakespeare's words expressing the despair of one who did not 'walk the tightrope' successfully, erring on the side of being too involved with institutional rather than spiritual affairs. In the play Henry VIII, at Act III, Cardinal Wolsey speaks to Thomas Cromwell, the King's Chancellor in the 1530s:

> O Cromwell, Cromwell: Had I but served my God with half the zeal I served my King, He would not in mine age have left me naked to mine enemies.

Chapter 14

Personal History and Contexts of Faith Nurture

At many points throughout this text on the maturing of faith, the *nurture* of the human spirit has been paramount. Threads of nurture in infancy, childhood and adolescence have widespread consequences concerning human life-course potential and outcomes, and not least upon our spiritual and faith development. Humans are an interdependent species, and *all faith is lived out in the context of webs of relationship.* Within this, the structure and dynamics of family life in their community contexts are understandably very important. Even in celibate monastic and convent settings, faith and life have to be lived out not in isolation, but in cheek-by-jowl communities of cooperation in which tensions are both natural and evident, however placid and calm the exteriors that tend to be assumed by those outside.

However, the word 'family' has become a controversial term in social and political discourse. There is a danger that an over concentration upon matters of family, important though they are, can prompt us to avoid facing the underlying issues and challenges of our personal faith, which are ultimately an *individual responsibility*. There can be no deep resolution of faith issues from behind the safe hiding place of benevolent family experience, or by using others who have wounded us by intention or neglect as scapegoats. Our families, however diversely structured, stable or unstable, are small communities of shared interests from which individuality emerges, for better or for worse.

While our birth and nurture within family settings provides the origins of our 'faith history', before we are influenced by wider social and institutional settings, ***each soul has to find its own self***. That is a crucial message of this text. Whatever our background history, life invites us to take our own journey; and that requires continuous resolve, courage, and the nurture of personal reflective capacities.

Of course this is not to minimize important matters of family dynamics and values, not least those between spouses, partners, mothers, fathers and grandparents that are so central for sustaining humanity and enabling young people in particular to thrive. Public policies may help or hinder these matters, but important though such issues are, and have been a focus in other writing by myself (and my editor), they are *not* my emphasis here.

All my experience tells me that personal faith can evolve, change and grow. That faith gradually unfolds if I as an individual let it happen, informing myself of the process on the journey. Then an unsurprising outcome is that all my relationships, not least with myself, are affected in generally positive ways. While I do believe that depth psychology can give us very important insights concerning ourselves and others (the work of Carl Jung and of Frank Lake are particularly important in that regard), it is important to recognize that personal faith cannot be psychologically induced by even well-justified social engineering. Hence all we can hope from the extension of so-called (and much needed) 'family-friendly' policies is that they may indirectly support journeys into faith development.

I need also to emphasize that even though I have long been an ordained clergyman, I am not particularly concerned here with matters of church organization and practice. However, I do believe that a truly alive and deepening church is one that engages and shares in some depth with families' complex and changing challenges over the life course; a rather rare feature in my experience.

Church worship and teaching can become far too habitual

without complementary depth in well-informed and sensitive pastoral practice. In this, sound ministerial formation is vitally important, yet too often misdirected. Spiritual formation was fundamental within the practices of Christ's ministry. As a good 'spiritual director', Jesus had that knack of asking just the right questions of those whom he encountered. It is sad to note that faith development of the kind that Fowler as an interdisciplinary scholar has outlined, without favor to any faith in particular, is rarely on reading lists for theological and ministerial formation.

14.1 Personal faith history reviewed

All of us have a personal faith history of some sort or other. Some are well developed, others are not; and all are to a large extent dependent upon our nurture. This nurture is not just specifically related to faith, but to our well-being in general. A bad, and sometimes abusive, nurture can bring about a very distorted and inadequate faith in adulthood. Experiencing negative faith nurture, or a nurture that ignores faith, may have disastrous effects upon people's faith development, and this is likely to be revealed in a wide variety of personal behavior. Therefore in seeking to understand faith and personal adjustment to life's ups and downs more widely, it is important for individuals to have a faith history that is generally sound from the outset. Without some articulation of personal history, debate or discussion about faith, or lack of it, within any individual is irrelevant, or even potentially destructive. Such can become playing games at a superficial intellectual level, not even touching at any point the true nature and importance of faith.

By way of review, there are *four* key issues that are important in considering a personal faith history. These are:

1. The maturity of an individual's faith bears no relationship to chronological age; neither does it relate directly to their intellectual ability or status in worldly terms. I have come

across too many cases of pensioners having a faith more immature than some teenagers. I have also met people who are highly trained professionals with a faith less mature than a person with no training at all. When a person has a soundly nurtured faith it is true that with age their faith becomes stronger, and a spiritual wisdom develops, but the faith must be there, soundly-enough laid in the first place. Relevant here is 'The Parable of The Talents' (St. Matthew's Gospel 25:14–30), noting that the word `talent' basically means 'the gift of faith'.

2. Next, is the related issue of appropriateness. In the New Testament the Greek word used for time is also relevant to faith development. Jesus always used the Greek word **XAIROS** when he referred to the time that was appropriate for something to happen. He often said, either, 'Now is the time,' or, 'The time has not yet come.' This is a word describing more than just the passing of time as expressed in the ticking away of the clock (chronos time). It is to do with a point when something is ready to happen, is 'timely', such as when fruit is ripe. Faith develops in people at different paces and in a wide variety of ways, rarely in step with chronological age. This makes truly focused pastoral care and faith nurture far more complicated than is usually recognized. It calls for obtaining a careful and thorough history of every aspect of an individual person's life before it is possible to have a reliable insight into their faith. For ourselves, we also need to know and understand our own faith history if our faith is to be fully nurtured into maturity.

As we have seen, faith is not primarily about having theories about life, and religion in particular, that are understood and sustained only at an intellectual level. Purely intellectual arguments about faith and religion may appear clever, knowledgeable, and even impressive to some people, but as far as understanding the faith of a person and developing it, such an approach is rather futile. The same applies to a legalistic approach that imposes a set of rules designed to create good behavior and good relationships. Faith is much more profound, involving the full nature of a person. No human being is a disembodied intellect. Our emotional nature is probably the most dominant, with evidence amassing concerning this from the emerging neurological sciences. So with confidence we can say that our emotions are the driving force behind intellect, not least in people who think that their intellect operates in a purely objective way. Room within mature outlook must therefore be found for conscience, will, active imagination and intuition.

3. Faith arises out of living relationships that are continually lived out on several levels, for faith lives within the essence of our whole being. It is about who we are as persons, how we view the world, and how we live. Faith must be nurtured by a rich range of relationships at every stage of our lives. The outstanding William Temple (Archbishop of York then Canterbury from 1929 until his too-soon death in 1944) noted in his great work, *Nature, Man and God*, that it was Rene Descartes' huge fallacy of 'I think therefore I am,' that prompted modern Western civilization to create many spiritual and emotional cripples. I would counter Descartes' narrow and destructive statement by saying, 'I have nurturing relationships, therefore I am.' The only constant factor is one of relationships, especially during childhood and adolescence. These relationships are many and varied, but the key ones are those with our mother and father as well as a few other significant people. These lay foundations from which other relationships become relevant. Those others can be of a wide variety, painful or joyful,

positive or negative, good or evil. Taken together they develop our faith and strengthen it as long as our key basic relationships are sound and, crucially, we feel reliably-enough loved. Where our key relationships are emotionally deficient or dysfunctional, then both seed and soil are likely to be far from optimum for faith to sprout, grow and be strengthened into maturity. Jesus' 'Parable of the Sower' is certainly relevant concerning this (see St. Matthew's Gospel 13:1–17).

4. Faith at its later and most developed stages becomes a powerful force in transforming our lives. I see in others and have experienced myself in my later years this sustained transforming power, which takes us beyond ourselves in such a way that we become more truly ourselves, seriously 'comfortable in our own shoes', and so more available and loving for others. As noted, for this to happen, we need to progress into the conjunctive stage, well beyond the seemingly safer yet anxious, fearful and fundamentally argumentative 'closed shop' synthetic-conventional stage.

When fundamentalisms of religious, scientific, philosophical, humanist, atheist and agnostic outlook predominate, they are symptoms of spiritual immaturity. No wonder that Jesus tells us not to be anxious and afraid, and that love overcomes fear, a closely related command. It is only when we are able to progress well beyond the synthetic-conventional stage of faith that we are even able to get a glimpse of true godliness and begin to see the futility of debate and dispute. The only way we can get this far is by being nurtured by love that in the first instance is of God. Again, Jesus said that unless our righteousness goes beyond the sort upheld by Scribes and Pharisees, we cannot gain spiritual peace, so entering 'the kingdom of heaven'; and the biblical word 'righteousness' means being in a right relationship with God, our fellow human beings and the whole of Creation.

14.2 Faith nurture and family life

Although I have emphasized that faith is ultimately a personal responsibility, the reality is that parents are every child's first teachers and role models. It is they who are most influential in shaping their offspring's attitudes towards formal educational provision, and almost all the associated learning outcomes. School-aged children in any case spend about 80% of their waking time at home and in their local community, so it is parents' implicit duty to watch carefully over them during those periods; to monitor and guide their use of TV, computers and so on, while keeping a watchful eye on the influence of their chosen friends and peer groups.

It is natural for parents to worry from time to time about the overall development off their offspring; this not least during the complex transition processes of adolescence when contemporary public educational norms of classroom work, tests and examinations are for many youngsters not the most helpful. Over that phase, when fresh hormones jingle, strong allegiances to peer groups often emerge, vying for attention beyond home's direct control. In this period, both values and faith are often seriously tested in the social marketplace. Wise parents hang on, taking care not to overreact through their own fears, while keeping sensitive and above all loving lines of communication open.

St. Augustine of Hippo, when recounting the time of his rebellious youth in his book *Confessions*, tells of how his mother worried about him, going to see the local priest for advice. The advice he gave her was to do nothing, other than love and pray for Augustine because as he matured he would grow beyond youth's excess.

Couples inevitably provide role models in varied ways of both male and female attributes. Sometimes these are distinctive in relation to gender, but oftentimes they are not, for each person of either gender embodies psychologically a varied mix of male and female traits. Those parents who value religious orientations will naturally view their particular relationships as having sacred dimensions, so are likely to endeavor to create a warm, habitually rhythmic 'church' within their home base. Family religion at best floods a home with light and insight, and welcomes guests of all ages in the same spirit.

This does not imply an atmosphere of pushy preaching, which is rarely the most appropriate way to demonstrate love and respect. Rather, qualities of warmth, availability and attentive, careful listening help both residents and guests to feel at home. There are clearly aspects of living in a state of both patient readiness and of spiritual composure, as Jesus did. Required is an atmosphere conducive to growth towards maturity. This is of course much easier said than done, but there is at least some truth in the saying that 'faith is more caught than taught'. A good life observed and propelled by inward faith is its own teacher, and sensitive parental nurture must never be confused with either instruction or emotional neglect.

14.3 Faith history in this life never ceases

With the hindsight of history, we know that much happens in the public square, and in churches, that is emotionally and spiritually adolescent. Perhaps many 'actors' of whatever status on the stage of life would be better served if ignored and were instead lovingly prayed for. Spiritual immaturity, not least among celebrity figures of diverse kinds, in which varied public projections become dominant, is a real form of sickness that too often is pounced upon and exploited by the mass media.

God is more than a projection of the human mind, but in the early stages of faith, as we have seen, projection plays a part in personality development. The Christian Gospel is a statement that, in the life of Jesus Christ, God comes to us in friendship just as we are, and wherever we are. This is in no way a human projection; rather a historical fact which begs our response. When we reach the point of being able to make our response, an active spiritual transformation can begin within.

As long as we inhabit this present world our faith history will always be incomplete. There is always more to come, and many more things which we do not yet know or understand, because our personal faith is a growing process. We do not know how, where or when it will end, so to keep faith alive we must keep journeying steadily on, not being knocked off course by any passing tidal waves. We also need to be in the companionship of others on this journey, and above all people who know from personal experience of the reliable Love of God.

Fortunately, there is now a wealth of faith-nurturing literature to help us, such as John Bunyan's *Pilgrim's Progress*, not forgetting a vast range of more recent texts, including spiritual poetry. A few specific suggestions are from page 233.

14.4 Some associated Bible readings

Finally, in summarizing the nature of faith and how it grows, I list below a selection of scripture readings that are relevant, inviting the reader to spend time pondering, reflecting and praying upon them. Faith nurture is not about giving people closed answers or formulae, but about giving food to nurture the soul, so that by taking it in and digesting it carefully, at our own speed, we may be strengthened.

Basic matters concerned with the revelatory character of biblical sources, essentially a mix of Old Testament *law*, the learning of the nature and practice of *love* throughout, and of *grace* emphasized in the New Testament, have been outlined previously. The Bible, when reflectively read, reveals the best and worst of human nature. The incompleteness of life in society, and the struggle to come to terms with the dark sides of human nature are there on raw display. Throughout all its component books, the Bible spells out a spiritual evolving and growth, pointing to 'a completeness' yet to come. The theme of faith, its nature and development, weaves through the texts like a golden thread in a complex tapestry.

In all Bible reading it is important that we do not get bogged down in the words themselves; rather to seek the truths that lay beyond them. If a text puzzles us or seems to mean nothing, advisedly we leave it, pray about it, and maybe come back to it later, when we may be moved on by the Holy Spirit in a 'ripe time'.

The Commended Biblical Textual Extracts

Old Testament

Genesis	Chapter 12 verses 1–9, Chapter 13 verses 17 to end, and Chapter 15 verses 1–21
Deuteronomy	Chapters 5 and 6
Isaiah	Chapter 53
Jeremiah	Chapter 31 verses 31–34

New Testament

St. Matthew	Chapter 5, and Chapter 13 verses 1 to 17
St. Mark	Chapter 8 verse 11 to Chapter 9 verse 13
St. Luke	Chapter 9 verses 18 to 26, and Chapter 24 verses 13 to 35
St. John	Chapter 1 verses 1 to 18, and Chapter 15 verse 18 to Chapter 16 verse 33
1 Corinthians	Chapter 1 verses 17 to 25, and Chapter 13 (printed in full on pages 231–2)
Ephesians	Chapter 4, and Chapter 6 verses 10–20
Hebrews	Chapter 11 to Chapter 12 verse 4
1 John	Chapter 4 verses 7–21
Revelation	Chapter 7 verses 9–17, and Chapter 21 verses 1–8.

Chapter 15

Epilogue – Faith, Hope and Love for the Future

I began by quoting the poem by Thomas Hardy called 'Dead Man Walking' (pages 13 & 14). I did so because it is a profound expression of the sickness in current Western culture. This is a sickness of spiritual and emotional emptiness in a time of material plenty and vast technical achievement. It is well said that despite all the perceived advances, intellectual achievements and affluence that was unimaginable a few centuries ago, those human beings who have the benefits of all these things are often left inwardly empty and feeling a sense of quiet, hidden, hopeless desperation.

As I travel around on trains and in the big cities, I hear and see constant noise and rush. I also see people wired up or wire-free with all sorts of gadgets that are products of modern technology, nodding away to kinds of sound that might have been familiar to people who worked in the dark satanic mills of an earlier century. This feels symptomatic of dead men walking, needing to cover up the emptiness expressed in the poem with noise. The deadness in so many people's faces expresses this; and human contact is marginalized. All these modern systems of communication communicate superficially, tending to dull or cover up the boredom of an inner emptiness.

This state of things concerns me mainly because as I have grown older I have lived outside such kinds of culture in a very different world. I am very happy with the world I live in, but at the same time I am very aware of this 'other world' because I live in parallel with it, and from time to time people from it come and talk with me. So I am very much in dialogue with that world, even though I do not like it and would not want to live within it myself.

However, I do have a considerable number of friends who inhabit my world and think and feel as I do. I also meet a good number of people of all sorts, many being strangers I bump into and have interesting conversations with, who also inhabit my world. Altogether there seem to be many who share the same general culture as me.

This experience suggests that modern Britain is a greatly divided culture. One senses that the division is less between genders or ethnicity than between 'dead people walking' and 'live people living'. That which divides is to a large degree a matter of faith and values. It is not a case of no faith or some faith, rather more a case of a faith that is adequate in enabling a person to be fully human and fully alive, or one that is inadequate and, in a modern phrase, 'not fit for purpose'.

I have now spent many years exploring the nature of faith, and, having presented what I have discovered, I wish to end with a conclusion that is positive in its basic nature. My grandchildren constantly remind me that although a good story contains bad things, because that is how life is, in the end good must always be victorious. I think this is a very healthy attitude. The predominance of literature and drama in which the final outcome is either a plain victory for evil, cynically negative, or inconclusive, further exemplifies the sickness of our times.

I have come to see faith as an essential aspect of human nature. Everyone cannot help but have faith in something that they perceive to be outside themselves. The issue is the nature of whatever or whoever it is in which our faith is rooted. Faith therefore is an unavoidable aspect of being human, but a faith in something that does not take us beyond ourselves but traps us and diminishes us, causing us to go round and round in ever decreasing circles, is more than inadequate; it is hugely destructive. It does not only destroy the individual by leaving them as 'dead people walking', it goes further, spreading out into a culture of easily disposable, fickle relationships, including the biophysical environment. In fact an inadequate or inappropriate faith is the outcome of idolatry. The whole of the biblical tradition, with all its complexities, of time, culture, language and place, consistently states that idolatry is a very serious matter because of its destructive nature.

Exploring this aspect further, *I suggest that faith in anything that does not take us outside and beyond the limits of our own mind diminishes both our vision and our creativity.* It greatly restricts our ability even to perceive the true nature of what is happening in the world around us. It limits our perceptions because we are reduced to a reliance on our own projections, and consequently the prejudices contained in them. The scientific humanist statement that 'Man is the measure of all things' is totally dehumanizing because it puts burdens on people that they cannot possibly bear. It excludes the well-established historical fact that things happen beyond the control or even possible imagination of mankind that deliver us and sustain us. It is a terrible burden to really believe that 'everything depends on me', so when things go awry 'I am therefore to blame'. Our present blame culture is a way out for those with this faith, that is, if they are devious and twisted enough to use it.

In his book, *The Earth in Balance,* Al Gore points out that the way we Western people have been conditioned to think about our relationship to the environment has contributed greatly to the current ecological crisis. In chapter 11 of that text he argues that there is an intellectual blindness or lack of perception behind the behavior that causes these problems. He sees a number of reasons for this, but traces their roots back to the philosophy of Descartes and the period called 'the enlightenment'. This caused a retreat into use of the intellect only as a means of understanding our world at the expense of the development of the whole person. The place of the arts, spirituality and the emotions have as a result become to a large extent marginalized. This in turn has led to massive increases in information which has now reached a point of overload. People have become so bogged down and exhausted by this that most cannot discern the false from the real, the valuable from the rubbish, and the relevant from the irrelevant. Because their faith has become rooted in the pressure to know all in what amounts to cultish information in order to succeed and perform in the culture it creates, there is no time to develop a faith that gives people the ability to rise above tidal cultural flows and become aware of all their flaws. Western man has, in short, become a victim of his own cleverness which is destructive of God-given sources of wisdom that would enable us all to have a positive and creative future. Only an adequate faith can restore this and change the dead man walking into a live man living.

The important point Al Gore makes, and relevant here, is that this whole culture of materialism and consumerism has created a blindness that is difficult to cure. There could well be many who might read this who could not discern what it is all about. They may well say that they have to live in the 'real world', and don't have time to consider these things, but Al Gore would reply that failure to do so, and as a result change our ways, is likely to lead to a disaster of unimaginable proportions. I would agree, and I believe we are close to the brink of such a disaster. However, a good awareness of history tells me that things beyond our control and understanding can happen, and there is always hope. It is faith that tells me this because it endows both awareness and vision to see beyond what now is. I also by the same faith see the present so-called 'economic crisis' as a blessing because it is an historical act forcing us back, if we are wise, to reality. I know many who think in terms of so arranging things that the present recession will eventually be over and the old ways will return. They will not. We have many more crises to come, but they will all give opportunity for blessings for those whose faith is sound and who have creative hope.

So I can conclude this text on a positive note, because as a person of faith I am realistically optimistic. A sound faith always gives hope, for through it we are enabled to have a vision that is greater than ourselves. We do not create this vision, but need to so discipline ourselves as to be in the right frame of mind and heart to receive it. Jesus said, 'Blessed are the pure in heart for they shall see God.' I have found this to be such a profound truth that it is the note on which I shall end.

What is meant by this 'purity of heart' and how is it achieved?

A pure heart is an attitude of mind that enables a person to feel so secure and childlike within the whole context of their environment that they are able to perceive realities that are beyond the material. This was well expressed by early 17th century Christian poet George Herbert in the following words:

> A man that looks on glasse
> On it may stay his eye
> Or if he pleaseth through it pass
> And then the heavens espy.

How can this be achieved? In short it cannot, because 'achievement' is the wrong word to describe the process. 'Achieve' is a word of modern man that means it is all down to making effort and using our own energy and cleverness. This approach only applies to material, technical objects, and so tends to destroy purity of heart by inner struggle and fear of failure. 'Purity of heart' as Jesus meant it is something that just happens within us as a result of good, well-balanced nurture that takes account of the whole person. In a predominantly materialistic world the surrounding culture militates against this, and as a result creates 'dead men walking.'

I conclude now by presenting the full text of what I consider to be the best written statement on the subject of a sound faith and the nature of its nurture in the whole world, and throughout the whole of history. It was written by St. Paul who stated clearly that he was the victim of an 'achievement culture' among his peers until a deep spiritual experience (on the road to Damascus) changed his awareness and enabled him to perceive a new reality. I believe those words of Paul are inspired because they are no projection coming out of the nature and experience of the man who wrote it, but from outside and beyond him.

Paul was thus a conduit for truth made possible by a sound faith. So 1 Corinthians 13 links three great virtues that are inseparable: Faith, Hope and Love.

St. Paul's First Epistle to the Corinthians, Chapter 13 [full text]

If I have all the eloquence of men and angels, but speak without love,

I am simply a gong booming or a cymbal clashing.

If I have the gift of prophecy, understanding all the mysteries there are,

And knowing everything, and if I have faith in all its fullness, to move mountains.

But without love, then I am nothing at all.

If I give away all I possess, piece by piece, and even if I let them take my body to burn it, but am without love, it will do me no good whatever.

Love is always patient and kind; it is never jealous; love is never boastful or conceited. Love is never rude or selfish; it does not take offence; and is not resentful. Love takes no pleasure in other people's sins but delights in the truth; it is always ready to excuse, to trust, to hope, and to endure whatever comes.

Love does not come to an end.

But if there are gifts of prophecy, the time must come when they must fail; or the gift of languages, it will not continue for ever. And knowledge… for this, too, the time will come when it will fail, for our knowledge is imperfect and our prophesying is imperfect;

But once perfection comes, all imperfect things will disappear.

When I was a child I used to talk like a child, and think like a child, and argue like a child; But now I am a man all childish ways are put behind me.

Now we are seeing a dim reflection in a mirror; but then we shall be seeing face to face. The knowledge that I have now is imperfect; but then shall I know fully as I am known.

In short, there are three things that last: faith, hope and love; And the greatest of these is love.

[Translation; The Jerusalem Bible, 1968 edition]

I was made to learn that biblical passage off by heart as a 13 year old grammar school boy. At the time I harbored resentment at having to do so, not least because I did not understand it. However, as an old man I have come to be thankful at being made to do that learning because I have the text firmly fixed in my mind. Time and time again I have been able to relate it to my own experience, meditate on it, relate it to other information and studies, marvel at it, and pray from it. The passage of time has slowly yielded a fuller understanding, and has emphasized for me the evils of our 'instant culture', which sadly seduces people down blind alleys.

That text does indeed open up new understandings to anyone who so desires. It helps me to be 'a live man living'. I hope and pray that all my readers may also find a similar outlook and confidence of a grounded and well-developed faith.

Sources for Further Reading

Editorial note

When asked about a short list of further reading suggestions, David was reticent about making recommendations. His reason is because he primarily hopes that readers will be encouraged to set off on their own explorations. David believes that 'faith', being its own entity, and involving the whole person, beckons such adventure. Furthermore, his experience suggests that those having an over-strong intellectual orientation can often avoid facing their whole selves by rationalizing away their emotions. Hence, for example, excessive entanglement with dimensions of theory, such as detailed terms within Fowler's, Erickson's and Kohlberg's writings, can for some be a distraction to the deepening of personal faith.

David thus sees his work here as primarily being for those who wish to take their spiritual pilgrimage seriously. He cautions about reading too much, and advises the seeking out of a friendly spiritual mentor, a mature person in matters of the inner life, as a guide on the road to spiritual growth, though he is well aware that such people are far too rare.

Nonetheless, 'further reading' is seen to have value, provided it penetrates beyond the intellect and superficialities of easy 'sound-bites'. David's hope is to deepen readers' spiritual roots within a valid tradition, aided by modern psychological insights.

The following sources are therefore commended as yielding fruit, provided each is approached in a prayerful spirit of contemplation rather than one of intellectual disputation. David notes that the Progoff and Silf books within this short list are related to practical personal journaling and to associated guided personal retreats that have deeply influenced his thoughts and prayers, the core resource that has produced this book.

RW

Sources for reference and further reading

St. Augustine, *The Confessions*, Oxford Classics, 2008, and *City of God*, Penguin, 2003.

David Bick, *Counselling and Spiritual Direction*, Pentland Press, 1997.

Gabrielle Bossis, *He and I*, Mediaspaul, 1988.

John Bunyan, *The Pilgrim's Progress*, Wordsworth Classics, 1996.

Erik Erickson, *Childhood and Society*, Norton, 1963.

James W. Fowler, *Stages of Faith*, Harper-Collins, 1981 (paperback 1995); also *Faith Development and Pastoral Care*, Augsburg Fortress, 1987.

Leslie Francis, *Faith and Psychology: Personality, Religion and the Individual*, Darton Longman & Todd, 2005.

Eric Fromm, *The Art of Loving*, Thorsons, 1995.

Harry E. Fosdick, *A Guide to Understanding the Bible*, SCM Press, 1958.

Al Gore, *The Earth in Balance: Forging a New Common Purpose*, Earthscan, 2007.

David Hay, *Something There: The Biology of the Human Spirit*, Darton Longman Todd, 2007.

St. Ignatius of Loyola: *Spiritual Exercises.* (There are a number of publications of these exercises from original to modern edited versions. Loyola University Press, Chicago is an authoritative source).

Philip Jenkins, *The Next Christendom*, Oxford University Press USA, 2007.

Lawrence Kohlberg, *The Philosophy of Moral Development*, Harper & Row 1981.

Frank Lake, *Clinical Theology: A Theological and Psychological Basis to Clinical Pastoral Care* (abridged edition, edited by Martin Yeomans), Darton Longman & Todd, 1986.

C.S. Lewis, *Selected Books*, Harper Collins, 2002 (includes *The Abolition of Man, Four Loves,* and *The Screwtape Letters*).

Rollo May, *Love and Will*, Norton, 2007.

Stephen Neill, *On The Ministry*, SCM Press, 1952.

Henri Nouwen, *The Return of the Prodigal*, Darton Longman & Todd, 1994.

Ira Progoff, *The Practice of Process Meditation*, 1980.

Eric Rayner, *Human Development*, Allen & Unwin, 1986.

Julia Segal, *Phantasy in Everyday Life*, Penguin, 1985.

Margaret Silf, *Landmarks: Exploration of Ignatian Spirituality*, Darton Longman & Todd, 1998.

William Temple, *Nature, Man and God*: *Christianity and the Social Order*, Penguin, 1956.

St. Teresa of Avila, *The Interior Castle*, (translation by Alison Peers), Wilder, 2008.

Anne Townsend, *Faith without Pretending*, Hodder & Stoughton, 1990.

Richard Whitfield, *Mastering E-Motions*, O-Books, 2005; & *Daring to Trust*, Face to Face Trust, 2011.

Editorial Afterword

As trusted editor, I have now reached a point of significant intimacy with David Bick's candid and creative text that goes way beyond the fortunes of friendship and into important re-ringings of uncommonly deep truth. Now each time I encounter this many-layered text at the various stages of proof-reading, fresh enlightenment dawns as my own problematic faith journey receives affirmations of what I can only term 'normality'. I believe that diverse others will find something similar happening should they have the good fortune and sense to persevere, without rush, with David's practical exegesis.

For example, I dare to sense that I now hover around Fowler stages 5 and 6, with glimpses of the ultimate stage of universalizing faith. Yet sadly, like many others, I scarcely learned anything of faith's progression within the diligent routines of parish church life and membership. This included preparation for the Anglican lay Office of Diocesan Reader, a role practiced for over 40 years in six English Dioceses.

Then beyond older, more respectful norms of academia, and the rough and tumble of child and family charities, in my final full-time appointment as Warden (CEO) of St George's House Windsor Castle, perceived by many in its early days as the 'Staff College' for the Church of England, I lived in a 'Royal Peculiar' context where pharisaic priestly attitudes of a local brand of power and control had for centuries been dominant. Thankfully, there are authentic forms of faith maturing for royals and commoners alike beyond such sad playpens of the wrong kinds of faith-immature group clericalism.

Hence I have come to believe that this text should become compulsory reading for all who seek to and are called to lead within diverse faith communities. David's book is both wise and practical. It is supported by balanced scholarship and has that rare, distinctive ring of challenge and inclusive truth.

Optimistically, there is increasing recognition that contemporary faiths, whether religious or secular, need to be viewed in the light of the scattered evidence of recorded history. Yet written history goes back at most a mere 10,000 years out of an evolving of life on our planet, now estimated at some 13 *billion* years since the mysterious vast energy 'big bang' that scientists hypothesize started off the Universe. We modern people wrongly tend to assume that humankind only became 'smart' with the emergence of Western-structured scientific insights, findings and then applications associated with the industrial revolution and beyond. Yet those were long preceded by important, yet now culturally marginalized insights in Persian, Polynesian, Greek and Roman cultures.

We need to learn afresh that 'cleverness' is far from being as deep as 'wisdom'. We are now faced, both scientifically and politically, with global threats to human existence on this amazing planet Earth. Now knowing that the planet's intertwined social and environmental ecosystems are unsustainable on their present dominant courses, somehow we must become re-birthed as 'maturely faithed world citizens' rather than 'global consumers'. Among the threats is widespread fear that faith-based cultural divisions between peoples will be a significant element within an impending holocaust of Armageddon proportions. So ours is indeed a truly 'pivotal era' in which a new equilibrium between ages-old oscillations of and tensions between matter and spirit, and so faith, must be found.

It is vital therefore that we understand more wisely the nature and nurture of faith that David Bick has charted in this text. His book is compiled from the wisdom and insights of both science, and of his own Christian religious tradition, whose Founder's central teachings, rather than the frail institutional arrangements of 'churches', are indeed revelations of eternal and universal truths.

This is all hugely relevant to what must become collective and radical changes in outmoded scientific and broadly 'theological' world views, recognizing that we are participating co-creators of possibility, rather than hapless victims of circumstance. The clear imperatives are to till and tend afresh the garden of Mother Earth, alongside the inner gardens of our delicate, yet often distracted souls, in every niche of our relational *inter*dependence.

While not getting bogged down in our 'sins', we must discover new synergies, viewing life as both our trust and an 'original blessing'. Any 'nirvana' or 'heaven' can only be made in the here and now through the devoted practice of compassionate and companionate faith, hope and love, well laced with our daring to trust and extending a generous forgiveness.

For love, not power or money, is the core, consistent, divine 'enlightenment' of all monotheistic faiths, attesting to a persuasive, collaborating non-coercive Creator. With the great gods of money and rampant materialism now becoming ethically and socially dethroned, we begin to recognize the ecological limitations to both economic growth and relational irresponsibility that infects the prospects of our living peaceably within the global village.

Zero growth in dominant macro economies, now globally essential, is only likely to be possible through the growth of faith-based, trustworthy multi-pronged relational respect. Truth and trust-based faith, with its clutch of distinctive stages, thus implicitly draws all our macro and micro politics towards the optimistic and coveted goal of global contentment. Any such nirvana will, however, fundamentally hinge upon the inner mature growth and development of faith, first within individuals in communities of trust, and then in societies and nations.

Richard Whitfield
Lyme Regis,
August 2010

A Note about the Face to Face Trust

It may have been noted on the reverse of the title page that the copyright of this text, ***Let Your Faith Grow***, has been vested by the author in the Face to Face Trust. The Face to Face Trust is a new evidence-based holistically-focused preventative educational charity, founded in 2008 [UK Registered Charity Number 1125105]. The word 'trust' in the title is viewed as an active noun, and amenable to significant enhancement through activity-enriched learning.

The basic business of the Face to Face Trust is *social trust-building*. More formally, it aims to advance the education of the public in the arena of inter-personal confidence, trust and relational reliability. This involves promoting the enhancement of self knowledge and the improvement of a range of life-skills, including effective couple and other human communication, and extending relational awareness and social competence.

Based upon the fundamental human necessity for diverse collaboration with others in trust, the basic 'glue' of any society, from family to nation, this aim lies within the broad vista of professional, workplace and community-related educational development in greatly neglected arenas of personal and relational formation, from childhood and beyond.

The Trust launched its website [www.facetofacetrust.org], and published an important basic book ***Daring to Trust*** (compiled by Richard Whitfield, Chairman of Trustees) early in 2011.

As resources permit, the Trustees have ambitious, yet realistic, grounded plans to fulfill the Trust's objects through conferences, seminars, workshops, organizational consultancy, supported by relevant, wide-ranging, informed and accessible publications.

The Trustees are most grateful to David Bick for endowing the Trust with the copyright and all royalties arising from the sales of this particular book. Human faith, whether secular or religious, goes seriously hand-in-hand with, and is indeed driven by trust. Naturally, the particular views expressed within this book remain the author's own, notwithstanding the textual influences of the editor.

O is a symbol of the world, of oneness and unity. In different cultures it also means the "eye," symbolizing knowledge and insight. We aim to publish books that are accessible, constructive and that challenge accepted opinion, both that of academia and the "moral majority."

Our books are available in all good English language bookstores worldwide. If you don't see the book on the shelves ask the bookstore to order it for you, quoting the ISBN number and title. Alternatively you can order online (all major online retail sites carry our titles) or contact the distributor in the relevant country, listed on the copyright page.

See our website **www.o-books.net** for a full list of over 500 titles, growing by 100 a year.

And tune in to myspiritradio.com for our book review radio show, hosted by June-Elleni Laine, where you can listen to the authors discussing their books.